T0148167

OUR GREATEST CHALLENGE

As we progress in life, reaching astounding heights in Power, Wealth and Fame ....

Moving our Greatness Beyond Mortal Limitations becomes our Ultimate Challenge ...

In the absence of a power to go on and on ... we are left with just one choice and gratification.

To create chronicles that will ....

"Leave back our names echoing across the planet for many centuries to come.

Elmo Ebert

WILL THE WORLD REMEMBER YOUR NAME?

An Evolutionary-Centered Philosophy

ELMO EBERT

ARCHWAY
PUBLISHING

Copyright © 2018 Elmo Ebert.

All rights reserved. No part of this book may be used or reproduced by
any means, graphic, electronic, or mechanical, including photocopying,
recording, taping or by any information storage retrieval system
without the written permission of the author except in the case of
brief quotations embodied in critical articles and reviews.

This book is a work of non-fiction. Unless otherwise noted, the author
and the publisher make no explicit guarantees as to the accuracy of
the information contained in this book and in some cases, names of
people and places have been altered to protect their privacy.

Archway Publishing books may be ordered through booksellers or by contacting:

Archway Publishing
1663 Liberty Drive
Bloomington, IN 47403
www.archwaypublishing.com
1 (888) 242-5904

Because of the dynamic nature of the Internet, any web addresses or
links contained in this book may have changed since publication and
may no longer be valid. The views expressed in this work are solely those
of the author and do not necessarily reflect the views of the publisher,
and the publisher hereby disclaims any responsibility for them.

Any people depicted in stock imagery provided by Getty Images are
models, and such images are being used for illustrative purposes only.
Certain stock imagery © Getty Images.

ISBN: 978-1-4808-6393-4 (sc)
ISBN: 978-1-4808-6392-7 (e)

Library of Congress Control Number: 2018947596

Print information available on the last page.

Archway Publishing rev. date: 06/26/2018

Perhaps, you are Powerful, Wealthy, Famous or certainly in the right direction to be there …

Capitalize on your strengths to shift your life and Profession to a new dimension that empowers you to transform the planet to a better place and it's people to a life of fulfillment.

TRANSFORM YOUR GREATNESS TO.....

"AN UNDYING LEGACY "

Elmo Ebert

Author's Note

I'm a "Conscious Evolutionnaire" impulsively taking control of my own evolution in terms of consciousness and intelligence.

As a "Visionary Writer" I'm platformed at a Mental elevation that empowers me in percieving the world with a higher state of logics and understanding. In this mental stature I find it extremely unprincipled to cite and progress by whats already known to us, of life and the dynamics around it.

I'm addressing my views to a few extra-ordinary individuals, and to those who are contemplating moving their work and life to a new dimension.

It excites me to shift my thinking and my way of writing beyond the conventional.

- *This book is not intended to step back to the past and inspire you with ostentatious writings of how a few remarkable individuals achieved astounding heights in life.*

- *It's not about mounting this book with a number of research findings based on past experiences to strengthen your beliefs and convictions in support of my thinking.*

- *It's not about "been practical", simple or laying down a few quick steps to accomplish Legendary heights in life.*

  Its Evolutional, Transformational and Meta-Cognitional, exploring the unknowns of life … magnifying our visions and attiring ourselves with an Adequate Mental Instrument to capture the invisibilities of life that can migrate us to a new dimension in Consiousness and Intelligence.

This "Evolutionary centered philosophy" helps and supports self directed individuals, Pioneers Creators and the bold and daring, to move their work and life to a new dimension empowering them to lead the world and its people to better, richer environments and to meaningful and fulfilled living.

Perhaps,it was your impulsive curiosity or that conscious or unconscious yearning to move your life and your work beyond the conventional that aroused you to know more about this book.

Read it, not simply to read and follow, but " *to consolidate your explorative thinking with that of mine* ......" You and I belong to a 'Community of A few Extra-ordinary People.'

Come Think with me ... *As a "Conscious Evolutionnaire" I engage myself in compulsive mental activities related to my growth in consciousness and intelligence beyond the rational.*

I firmly believe that my work is of an infinite nature ... which for many more centuries to come will help and support individuals to take a positive transformation, living a more meaningfull and purposeful life.

Elmo Ebert.

RACE YOUR MIND.

Biological complexities, neurological refinement(brain) and consciousness are counterparts in the growth and development process of an individual ... they are interdependent for effective functionalities. The question is when it comes to the point of saturation of the growth and energy levels of our bodies ... this whole development process slows down to ultimately end up with a total breakdown when the body cannot sustain itself.

Imagine what growth and development could take place in terms of neurological refinement and consciousness if this integrated power sustained itself together for a 200 or 300 years.

The key point here is that we have got the liberty,the power to race our minds ahead of this combination. We don't have the power to accelerate biological growth ... that's a natural growth process and a natural waning process ... but we do have the power to develop our brains and minds ahead of our bodies ...... not waiting for nature ... but nurturing its growth.

"*We choose to be great, not because the road to greatness is an easy pleasurable drive ….but because it is winding, and a tuff terrain right to the top.*"

Elmo Ebert

A dedication to …

My Mother, Mary Anne and my Father, Walter Emil, who has tran-
scended into a new dimension in life, that remains a mystery incomprehensible at our present levels of Consciousness and Intelligence..

CONTENTS

Part 3—Guiding The Planet And Its People..

THE NEW AGENDA

I will not bore you filling many pages of this book with detailed past stories and facts of some of the greatest people in the planet who with their visionary thinking and legendary accomplishments have thrust the world to what it is today with all its splendor and great living environments ...... and some of the largest Corporates who recorded astounding heights in overall growth and development with high emphasis on Innovation and Evolutionary Centered Thinking. Instead, I have tossed out a few important guidelines of what, ideally it means to move our work and life to a new dimension.

So What's a new dimension in life and in work ...

Primarily let's take life ...

Moving your life to a new dimension is a migration into a new state of consciousness and Intelligence ...... attired with *An Adequate Mental Instrument* to perceive, comprehend and capture the world with a higher sense of logics and understanding and through a wider dynamical zone than our five sensory footprint. In this sense we recognize and even engage our non-physical faculties for progressing with Human potentials such as Intuition, precognition clairvoyance and other powers that are treasured beyond the powers of the physical mind.

NOTE:

The term non-physical mind does not imply something of a paranormal nature or some psychic phenomena ...... It is in real fact the Highest State of Consciousness that we can reach in our organic scale. A stage where our minds have developed to the extent of capturing data from beyond our physical sensory capacities ...... It is essentially different from the four basic entities of space, time, energy and matter of the conventional science ...... It is endowed with Autonomous will and the power of creation, retention and obliteration of beliefs and knowledge of an individual.

This new Cognitional Faculty empowers you to sense,see aspire and achieve astounding accomplishments beyond the reach of an ordinary Mental faculty.

This is not a spiritual or paranormal transcendence, but an elevation to the highest state of consciousness within our organic scale.

In our Professional engagements we are going beyond the accomplishments of Power, Wealth & Fame ...... Our focus here is of a Humanitarian nature. Whilst holding on to our visions and missions in whatever is our Profession we are moving our energies and efforts in contributing constructively toward the betterment of the whole of humanity along with positive changes in the Economic, Social and Political affairs of the Planet. You'll only see it as an obligatory and praiseworthy task when you have moved your life to this new levels of cognition.

In view of the present issues that the world is facing ...... The world is in need of SUPER-LEADERS ...... Leaders who has the capacity to think not "outside the box ... but ' beyond the rational Mind, beyond pragmatic thinking skills.

We have seen many addressing these issues for many decades with not much success, perhaps perceiving worldly problems with an ordinary state of logics and understanding.

Moving your work to a new dimension means guiding and directing the world and its people with the integrated strengths of your Extraordinary Intellectual abilities and your rich Material possessions and dignified recognition.

WHEN you carry the past to the future you are building a future on a past foundation ... getting better and better in what you already know. The future here is of a more horizontal nature in growth and development. Yes! We need to get better and better in what we have and we do, which has taken the world forward ... giving us better and richer environments and opportunities for better living ... however it is Innovation, Creation and designing that has thrust the world forward to what it is today.

Unlike building the future by encompassing your past ... When you turn-off the past and move to the future you are innovating, inventing a future ... discovering the unknowns. This is the true meaning of moving your life and your work to a new dimension.

To invent a future you need a liberalized mind detached from the influence and interference of your existing knowledge and life's experience, beliefs and convictions, your ego-driven attitude. You need to be a visionary with foresight, precognition and to exercise your liberty to think abstract, illogical ... to hypothize extrapolate, before you discern that they are imperceptible or elusive ...

In this new dimension ....

- You will mentally advance yourself from a five sensory to a multi-sensory Individual ... in the sense that you will also encompass non-physical realities as part of your growth and development process.

- You will grow in mental-psychic clarity and will make personal and Business decisions based on intuitional promptings as well as rationality.

- You'll understand psychological growth as evolutionary and develop methods and institutions not just to cure emotional disease but foster the growth of consciousness.

- You,ll see basic Education, Corporate Education and personal growth and development as a discipline in moving to higher stages of consciousness ... and re-construct educational, Corporate and personal GROWTH THEORIES and institutions accordingly, with special emphasis on personal hierarchic development.

- You'll use mass media, instant telecommunication and human/computer linkages as vehicles of bonding consciousness and unity.

- You'll Re-define and Re-write the Principles of Business Management embracing the vertical growth of consciousness as a strategic constituent part of a Innovative Business mechanism powered to move business efficiencies and growth potentials to unimaginable heights.
- You' ll lead and guide the world and it's people to live a more meaningful and purposeful life

You need to be bold and daring in your thinking and have the courage to shoulder any type of criticism before you see and feel the glory and ecstasy of your innovations.

That passion and yearning for legendary accomplishments resides in all of us. And hidden deep within us unconsciously is that craving for immortality ... for that gratification to go on forever. The more we succeed, the stronger is this desire. Our greatest challenge is to remain perpetual along with our achievements and our possessions.

We will move mountains, if we are rewarded with the liberty to remain immortal. Instead, we remain with just one choice ....

"To leave back our names echoing across the planet for centuries to come ....

This could be achieved by moving our work and our life to a new dimension ... where the glory and ecstasies of success transcends material limitations.

There are no social, financial standards, academic principles or disciplines that governs legendary accomplishments ......

You can leave back a legacy, born and living in the most underdeveloped environs or studying in the most sophisticated academy in the world ... this empowerment comes from the greatest academy in life ... and that academy is deep within you.

Let me welcome you to a bold and daring journey in search of our undiscovered cognitive instruments that will thrust our life to a higher state of consciousness, logics and understanding ... let's make a responsible choice to move our professions and our life to a new dimension empowering us to continue the glory of our great accomplishments beyond its material boundaries.

Submerged deep within us is an aggressive challenging attitude. Characteristically we want to be Intellectually Invincible. We face adversities overcome challenges bravely and are attired to face the most extreme challenges of all.

We don't intend transcending to a supernatural state ...... but we do have what it takes, to bravely say! ....

"Yes I intend to continue serving the planet and its people for many more centuries to come, in my own chosen way."

If what we are pondering and pursuing ... dosen't seem like crazy to the rest of the world ... perhaps, we are in a delusion.

"Audaciously Creating the Difference"

"As we migrate into this new dimension ideas such as "Liberty" or "Equality" or a "Classless Society, perhaps, take root within us …… visualizing a new world of meaning, value and fulfillment to all mankind.

"Once it is expressed, it will be absolutely difficult to be detached from it. It acts like a new dimension in thought which may transcend the realm of our present thinking. Essentially in this great Vision are many components that perhaps may not be purely cognitive."

INTRODUCTION

As the world evolves from one stage to another many facts that were established in the past seems obsolete. Even The Big Bang Theory is questionable today.

As we move along with growing biological complexities and neurological refinement ... alongside we grow in consciousness ... we see and sense more and more of life and the universe. If we are to Guide and lead the world we need to be working with extra sensory mental instruments sensing the world with pre-cognitive abilities ... not leaving our dependency on only the known facts of Life.

A few individuals will lead this new era, elevating themselves to a higher level of logics and understanding to face these new challenges. They will lead the world and its people to a new dimension in meaningful and purposeful living.

I Feel great to be a part of this bold exploration. Inspired now and again by intuitional promptings and subtle connections to my Higher Intelligence I've turned Philosopher, out of a non-scholarly background which drives me from the inside into an intrepid explorative Mission ... A Mission to create "An Evolutionary Centered 'Philosophy For Greatness'. It will inspire me and give me immense pleasure to be recognized and take me as what I'm today.

NOBODY is the ultimate expert in the Science of successful living. Many have been given the liberty and the genius to be an expert only on certain constituent parts of this undiscovered mysterious Principle.

Someday in the future we will be able to bring all these expertise together, maybe, through a medium of shared consciousness. Until that day, let each of us do what we can to help and support Men and Women to reach their destinations in life, irrespective of the fact whether they are Spiritual or material goals.

I'm driven into this exploration by the belief and conviction that we have not as yet discovered our total Potential and true Principles that governs Extra-ordinary achievements in life. Our growth and development aspirations and accomplishments in life depends on many factors.

Reaching legendary heights in whatever we do requires an explorative Mind in search of all our constituent mental faculties, Knowing their functionalities, their influences' and their levels of contribution towards our pursuits in life.

In addition to the relevant competencies and skills required to do a job efficiently, in the process of implementing a task there comes into play the dynamics around each and every part of our whole being, physical and mental, and even certain forces at work beyond Mind and Body.

Beginning from an individuals' Evolutionary progression, unconscious intentions, your Subconscious Mind, perceptions, beliefs and convictions and even perhaps non-physical faculties and realities such as, intuition, instinct etc ... plays a role in all our efforts and endeavors in life.

Legendary accomplishmenst are inevitable when its driven with the integrated power of our total mental faculties. Although all external fundamental factors such as a proper plan of work and the required resources are available and are in place working toward an end result ...... *An individuals' inner state of affairs could very well jeopardize the expected outcome of any project or errand, if the physical and mental faculties are not moving in one direction in partnership and harmony.*

My Aim is to orchestrate this partnership and harmony and write out a Philosophy disseminating this 'know- how ' to help and support people to aspire and realize in life ...... what seems an impossibility as at now.

The mental weaponry that we use to battle today have lost its competitive edge ... perhaps they should be left behind paving the way for the creation of a new kind of weaponry that will move us to a higher level of consciousness, intelligence, and abilities.

Its time for the emergence of a new vocabulary that addresses the world from a higher stand-point in mental stature.

This book is meant to build an indomitable foundation with our intrinsic faculties and external conscious efforts moving in the same direction that will empower us to construct a new mental architecture and an adequate cognitive instrument to move our life and professions to a level that empowers us to accomplish legendary heights in all our pursuits in life.

The methodology used in helping and supporting the reader to reach its intended goal,is not presented through the traditional means of a step by step progression, but by a self directive approach that convincingly builds beliefs in one's true potentialities, initially arousing intellectual curiosities and comprehension that will lead to actual practice in this interest.

If I did follow a conventional or traditional method of attempting to introduce this book to you, then right from the start I'm contradicting my own convictions and beliefs that we need to theorize, conceptualize and share knowledge exercising our liberty detaching ourselves from the past. Lets Use our liberty our choice boldly and confidently rather than been caged and judged in the ways that things have been done conventionally and traditionally.

This book is not meant for you to simply reflect on what's said or follow certain guidelines, but to consolidate your exploratory thinking with that of mine.

So let me welcome you on- board a vessel that will pierce into the unknowns of life giving us better insight inspiration and intelligence to perceive the world with a higher level of consciousness empowering us to protect the planet and guide our people to a fulfilling and purposeful way of life.

What is of paramount interest is the power of your Autonomous will and choice to penetrate into the unknowns of life to discover new horizons that will empower you to move your work and life where only a few extraordinary individuals belong.

"Beginning's of great explorations in life, most times, were never perfect; Accepting that fact and working towards perfection is a perfect beginning".

Elmo Ebert Dubai Winter *2017*

Re-Defining A Legend

Legendary accomplishments needs to be re-defined. There's what should be termed as GREAT and what should be acknowledged as LEGENDARY.

There are **great** achievements within the reach of every individual such as a great Political Leader a great scientist, a celebrity or a great athlete ... however Legendary accomplishments are beyond greatness and beyond the glory of Power Wealth or Fame ...... it requires a higher state of consciousness and intelligence above the ordinary, and An Adequate Cognitive Instrument to sense perceive and capture the world with an higher level of logics and understanding, and from a wider dynamical zone than that of our five sensory footprint.

Legendary accomplishments are not self centered ... in the sense that it does not focus energies on one,s own self but has a humanitarian inclination towards bringing solace to the whole human race.

legendary accomplishments are beyond the bounds of Power Wealth or Fame ... An individual can be recognized as a legend, when what has been accomplished has created a positive impact, not just to a few people within his control ... but to the lives of all men and women living in this planet, irrespective of the fact whether they are from the east or west rich or poor black or white.

Let's hold the GREAT'S with high respect and admiration ... and THE LEGENDS as A few Extra-ordinary Individuals who transformed this world to a better place to live.

PART 1

Into a New Dimension

Past presidents are forgotten, *Forbes'* billionnaires are forgotten, and most greats in power, wealth, and fame are forgotten ...

It's not about being remembered for hundreds of years. It's about something much greater.

- It's about being content and feeling that the glory of the hard work and sweat over many years, which have given you high financial and social stature, is worthy of undying recognition.
- It's about guiding the world with the inexpressible drive that triggered and thrust you from deep within to who you are today.
- It's about how you missed out on the true glories and values of life in the pursuit of that voracious desire for power and wealth ... then sharing these experiences with the world.
- It's about sharing your wisdom to direct and guide the world through a philosophy that can transform the whole human race to encompass humanistic values and live lives of true meaning and purpose.

If leaders of great nations merged their thinking, pooled their national resources, and joined hands to identify and address worldly issues instead of attempting to overpower each other using colossal amounts of money, time, and brains for nuclear defence and other combat weaponry, today's world would experience something better than an imbalanced 80/20 control scale.

Lead the World

To lead in grandeur, you need to sense, see, and capture what's beyond others' reach.

To be empowered with this belief, this visibility, and possibility, you should elevate yourself to a higher level of consciousness, intelligence, and ability.

- Elmo Ebert, conscious evolutionnaire

A DARING ADVENTURE

We are all born as part of the human family, the human species, with the same metabolism and anatomical conception. Genetics do play a role in shaping and fashioning our personalities but eventually to get wiped out by the most powerful craftsman of our personality—our beliefs and convictions. These are built up along with levels of education, knowledge, and the influences of the environments we live in. The personalities we dispose of are not by chance or choice, but mostly by circumstances.

Our beliefs and convictions were built on external influences, such as where we stood socially and financially.

In this socially and financially imbalanced world we find many struggling in the heavier seat of the scale. Emerging out of this imbalanced scaling, there were a few extraordinary individuals who refused to accept external circumstances as determinants of their future. They searched the depths of their inner-most self where external influences had no effect.

Throughout history, we have witnessed the greatest people belonging not just to a particular community or society, political or financial standing, but they came from everywhere—from the most uncivilized places or from a noble family or a farmer's son.

Irrespective of what profession you are in—a psychologist, scientist, businessman—it's best to think of yourself as an individual looking at new ways of thinking about your profession, thus giving your role a new definition and taking it to a new dimension. Great minds are explorative, looking in every direction and rejecting no possibilities.

An indisputable fact about great people is the power of their beliefs in their innovative and creative thinking, coupled with their daring attitudes towards discovering the unknown.

Moving your life to a new dimension needs something more than knowledge and education, skills and competencies, talents or physical advantages. It requires

- an indomitable mindset,
- a balanced and unwavering disposition,
- an autonomous choice and will,
- a positive attitude to pioneer, originate, and explore, and
- a creator needs liberty for hypothesis and extrapolations in the absence of facts.

You can read, listen, and watch a hundred or more stories and facts that are inspirational. But just as the greats tell us, "Genius is 10 percent inspiration and 90 percent perspiration."

This whole gigantic universe is in continual movement, like a colossal vessel moving the whole of nature toward a meaningful destination that still remains only within the comprehension of a supernatural being.

Many of our past generations have been on board this vessel moving from one stage to another in terms of consciousness, intelligence, and ability, just like you and I are on board today, comprehending this journey a little better than our forefathers did.

These movements are bringing about continuous changes in the world of minerals and life forms, such as plants, animals, and the ultimate life form—humans. We consistently grow in consciousness.

I'm of the strong belief that it should be our ultimate quest to put all our energies into understanding what we are biologically, temperamentally, and constitutionally, not perceiving us only as individuals but as members of the human species. I believe this will inspire us to aspire higher and higher in worldly accomplishments and spiritual attainments.

We will leave the relevant experts to guide us in the relationships we have with the rest of nature. Today we must focus on discovering our full potential.

If we are to explore the ultimate in human potentialities, we have got to think not simply outside the box but beyond the physical capacities of the mind.

Primarily we need to get over this fundamental problem of misconceiving that anything beyond physical realities are paranormal, occult, or completely insensible to be putting efforts and energies into discovering them. Instead, it's time that we accept and acknowledge the fact that although we are unable to provide scientific evidence about the existence of non-physical realities, they do exist. Religion tells us so.

I don't feel at ease or content simply considering myself as merely a verifier of scientific facts. What excites me is to speculate freely, to theorize, and to explore into the unknowns of life. I'd prefer to come under a heavy hammer of criticism rather than sit by a stream and watch the rest of the world toiling to show me the true meaning of life and its full potentialities, convinced that great achievements are beyond my reach. I wish to apply my existing knowledge to discover new knowledge, disseminating it to bring more value to people.

In this life's movement there are participants and spectators. Win or lose, perfect or imperfect it is the participation that should drive us to be better intellects and better perceivers of life and the dynamics surrounding it.

Explorers of life are generally lonely but very courageous people, all the time struggling with inner conflicts, fears, and even paranoia. Some great people even risk their professional recognition to present their personal assertions.

We should not attempt to erect barriers between what states of consciousness are required for spiritual purposes and what is for material gain. Instead, we should serve one another and find ways of integrating these powers to engage them for the purpose of our choices.

"You have arrived at a point in life, a point at which it's not inspirational citings or stories or motivational quotes or writings or seminars that drive you further or create an impact in your life. You are looking for new intelligence, new abilities that could move you to higher stages of logic and understanding ... higher in a consciousness that differentiates you from the rest, thus empowering you to an extraordinary level of self-esteem and a worldly recognition that's beyond the glory of wealth, power, or fame."

Elevating yourself from where you are today into a higher stage of wealth or recognition is well within your reach. But what matters most to you today is to discover a map and a path so you might move yourself and your work to a dimension that's not within the reach of an ordinary mind or individual.

You are searching for something beyond the boundaries of knowledge, intelligence, and normal abilities. Mostly you are caught up with your routine engagements, unable to progress with this hidden desire that triggers you now and again.

This discipline to release yourself to spend some time in the greatest academy of life, which is located at the zenith of your mind, is an uncompromising responsibility if you are to realize these great aspirations in life.

You have reached a point of success as you get better and better in what you do and what you know. Your intentions, thoughts, and actions are directed toward what you are presently engaged with. Life has moved you to an obsession caging you in and depriving you of the opportunities for exercising your aptitude and power for innovation, creation, and the passion and desire for pioneering.

Lead the world just as you are leading your business conglomerate and its people. You've got much more in you. Let yourself loose to unleash the genius in you.

Move your life and your work to a new dimension. Guide the world to a more meaningful and purposeful living.

A Few Extraordinary Individuals

It takes more than courage and a daring attitude to change conventional or traditional ways of thinking and doing things. A few extraordinary individuals dared shift their thinking and pushed boundaries, migrating to new horizons in discovering, understanding and exploring human potentials and possibilities. They changed the world for the better, creating more meaning and value, building richer and safer environments, and transformed the world to more like one human community. They connected people from all corners of the planet to help and support each other when the need arose, irrespective of whether they were black or white, or they came from the East or West. These great names still echo across the planet and will go on for many more centuries into the future.

Shifting our thoughts to a new dimension means challenging our own existing beliefs and convictions, perceiving and analyzing the world and everything in it with a higher level of logics and understanding, despite the fact that they may seem out of reach in the beginning.

In simple terms ......

"To be bold enough to make change, is to dare undo yourself, your source traits. Its a RE-THINKING, RE-DEFINING and RE-PROGRAMMING exercise of your levels of consciousness and intelligence ...

Most of all making this change requires a tough mind to face its challenges, even transitional adverse consequences ... before experiencing its amazing ecstasies.

No matter 'Who You Are' or Where you stand in social, financial or Academic standards as at today … Take a bold transformation in life.

Exercise your greatest gifts in life "Your liberty" "Your Autonomous Choice & Will" to leave back a Legacy. This gift is indestructible and inaccessible to the rest of the world.

Legendary aspirations and destinations never was impeccably visible in the beginning they all saw it as if fogged and veiled with mystery..as you move deeper and deeper with unblemished attentiveness everything becomes crystallized, your visions magnified, your perceptions broader, you are attired with a new cognitive instrument to take control of your own evolution. At these higher levels of mental stature, what seemed like an impossibility becomes possible.

Legendary accomplishments are not only judged by how powerful, wealthy or famous you are … But more by what wisdom moral values and a higher level of logics and understandings that you have imparted to the children of earth … to help and support them in all their pursuits … Irrespective of the fact whether they are intended for material gains or spiritual attainments.

You can do this in the comfort of a luxurious mansion in a metropolis … or in the simplicity of a country cottage.

Either way. "**The World Will Remember Your Name**"

We are a continually evolving Human Species, ever changing in biological complexities and neurological refinement all the time … and this is an unconscious natural process.

WE HAVE GOT A CHOICE …… TO LET US GROW IN INTELLIGENCE AS A NATURAL PROCESS … OR TAKE CONTROL OF OUR OWN EVOLUTION AND NURTURE OUR GROWTH.

Nobody is the ultimate expert in discovering, defining or actualizing the ultimate potentials and powers of the human being … it is proven that the mind in association with the human brain is the most complex and paradoxical device in all nature …… and remains indefinable … incomprehensible despite many attempts made by many experts for centuries.

The very fact that we remain an unexplored life form in terms of potentials ... tells us that there is an element of a mysterious nature, unlimited capacities and potentialities lying undiscovered within us.. ... after all if we do have limited capacities and functionalities like an artificial machine does.. ... then we can be specifically defined.

We can express ourselves to a great extent in a biological and neurological perspective ... but if one is to ask the true meaning and purpose of this integrated human system along with its brain ...... with trillions of inter-connected elements of neural wiring ...... Now that seems a difficult one to answer.

In this sense the approach toward life, in the positive, should be, not to shut us from perceiving life by only that which is known to us ....but by moving forward with the liberty to presuppose that we are a species with unlimited potentialities ....although they seem beyond understandings as at now. Perhaps our primitive dull faculties will someday evolve to the extent that we see us in total completeness. Until such time let us boldly adventure to take us to a new dimension in our efforts and energies in whatever we do.

I strongly believe that the scientific study of life or an architecture to achieve greatness does not require a model of science that we inherit from physics, chemistry or astrophysics. In exploring the Science of successful living or the road to legendary accomplishments, we should have the liberty to extrapolate even looking at the mysteries, the ambiguous and all other aspects of existence that seem difficult to communicate.

We drive ourselves into the unknown ... inspired by our beliefs and heroism and our strong convictions that we are governed and controlled more by the unknowns of life than the facts known to us. It's not when you are with the crowd that the world will rise to applaud you ... but when they realize that you have broken away to extraordinary levels ...... mentally attired with an adequate instrument that can perceive the world with a higher level of consciousness, that empowers you to discover new human possibilities ... which seem impossible and incomprehensible to an ordinary state of mind.

Power Wealth and Fame can draw obedience ... can draw dependency and admiration ... but they cannot change minds..

Come with me let's take control of our own evolution. Only a Few Extraordinary People can sense this possibility.

'The most unacceptable devaluation of life, is to <u>REFUSE</u> to see the positive visibilities of life ... And REJECT to pursue whats' possible'

Elmo Ebert

<u>Nurture Your Own Evolution.</u>

When you are in control of your own evolution your intellect grows at an unimaginable and unpredictable pace beyond that of an ordinary individual, empowering you to aspire and reach legendary heights in Life.

Elmo Ebert.

"The Power we command cannot subjugate the whole world … The Wealth we posses cannot fulfill all our material desires and the Fame we celebrate does not touch the hearts of every human being.

Legendary accomplishments are performed at a level of Consciousness and intelligence that supersedes the grandeurs of Power Wealth and Fame with its glory and values generously accessible to every human being across the planet."

Elmo Quotes.

An Infinite Recognition

Success' ultimate destination is to pass on its values and glory for many centuries to come. Attempting to reach these astounding levels of greatness through extrinsic motivational factors or stimulants and injunctions such as passion,commitment dedication is a vain effort. Shifting our success stories beyond its material boundaries, primarily, requires a quantum shift in our thinking beyond its present limitations.

An accomplishment can be asserted as "LEGENDARY" only if its architecture,engineering and construction required intelligence beyond that of an ordinary mind.

Legendary accomplishments needs to be redefined. Many greats have been sweating in mind and body for many years in their life to move the world to richer and better environments giving people opportunity to live a good fulfilling life and build a stable future. They worked untiringly to reach astounding heights in life ... but most unacceptably all whats done moved into nothingness along with life's mortal destiny.

"Legendary achievements should be given an infinite recognition and the power to sustain its positive vibrations for many centuries to come."

Its time the world Redefined the true meaning of a legacy ...... As long as we are caged within the boundaries of this "thinking prison" we remain with the crowd.

Its time we take a bold transformation in life acknowledging the fact that we belong to a community of a few extraordinary people who are of the belief and conviction that we do have the required cognitive instruments to link ourselves to our higher intelligence, and our mission should be to find the links that connects us there.

This does not mean that we have got to indulge ourselves in meditative acts or mystical contemplation. Primarily let us acknowledge the fact that we can move to higher levels of consciousness, intelligence and abilities when working as an whole rather than in isolation with constituent parts of our mental faculties. It is not looking for a scientific explanation or a logical rationale behind this, but instead expanding our perceptions,magnifying our visions to the extent that we see this existence. What seems non-existent becomes existent as we expand ourselves to that extent..

My point here is that we are the ultimate in creation, in possession of all required tools to explore our fullness which has its physical and non-physical realites. However, we mis-conceive this creation has one part of our faculties dedicated for material purposes and the other for spiritual purposes and we strive for success in material desires detached from our total self.

I wish I had a simple few steps to get you reach there ...... reach heights that only a few extraordinary people would dare ... but I don't and I don't believe simplicity and a few success steps or a few changes in habits will move us to a new dimension in our work enabling us to perform astonishing results beyond the capacities of an ordinary mind.

As we agree the road to Greatness is dark and winding ...... only a few are privileged to reach the summit ...... We are today moving the definition of Success 'outside the box 'giving success an undying recognition.

We are still changing biologically ... evolution goes on ... and our social-cultural evolution is proceeding at an extraordinary pace and destined for still more staggering acceleration in the decades ahead.

I believe that curiosity,the use of the mind,the craving to understand us in totality, the physicals and the non-physicals surrounding life, is the controlling difference between the men of the past and the men of the present era.

A New Age, A New Realization

Comparatively with a few decades ago Human nature today is changing at an extra-ordinary pace. A new kind of humanity is coming into existence, especially trends arising from science and the urge toward discovering of our own identity.

These dramatic changes are resulting in a world system of deeper and deeper complexities creating, an environment so challenging that the need for a new kind of intelligence and abilities becomes a categorical imperative ... to confront these changes. Perhaps, we may need a mental faculty that could capture data beyond our five sesory footprint and process them with a higher level of logics and understanding which is beyond the capacities of our ordinary mind.

From the beginning of the twentieth century these changes continue incessantly bringing development in all areas, undoubtedly, and also along with it immense psychic pressure to human lives.

The movement into a deeper and deeper complex world mechanism is also pushing severe changes in the life's of many, be it a great nation, an underdeveloped country,a community of political or business leaders or an individual. Just like the wave that hits the shore aggressively and forcefully, impacted by the shake up in the great ocean, everybody feels the vibration of this movement directly or indirectly. ..Holding onto traditional ways of thinking and perceiving the world could leave some of us way behind when confronting these incessantly changing challenges in life.

We are at the threshold of a new age ...... an age that will bring in new realizations new intelligence and new abilities. There will be pioneers who will migrate and discover new cognitive instruments empowering them to lead the world and its people to realize this evolution.

We join hands with the greats. We want to be a part of this great voyage, than leaving this task only in the hands of a few extra-ordinary people who are even today working laboriously towards making known the unknown.

We should support our fellow men to explore and explore this vast gigantic field of human possibilities moving the world and its people to richer, better environments and a fulfilling living.

In this sense, I feel the greatness of been a part of this bold exploration that I have embarked on ... and I'm certain you will share that greatness with me now that you are a part of this extra-ordinary community of people.

Some of our belief systems have imprisoned us, destroying our positive heroic attitudes towards life. We are all part of the same species no matter what extrinsic differences ... our inner human concept is made up of the one and the same metabolism giving us equal opportunity to think, analyze, act and be what we want to be ...... Our rationalistic logical minds are fracturing in confrontation with aggressive, unforeseen challenges in this fast changing environment. It's an heroic deed to be putting in all our energies and effort in discovering an adequate cognitive instrument which lies beyond the boundaries of the mind ... so that we may realize our full potentialities through the engagement of this extraordinary mental faculty.

There are so many tantalizing indications of something beyond the edge of everyday understanding ... that it seems a worthy and justifiable effort to engage ourselves in the study and development of these areas and analyze the effect it has on our success stories and not cowardly push them all aside as mere fantasy, hallucination or superstition.

"We should attire ourselves mentally with the required tools to perceive life's magnificent kingdom of possibilities, not as a mystery, but as a reality."

Primarily there is a great barrier that has to be hurdled to move forward. Minds will have to change bringing changes to belief systems, value systems, attitudes and perceptions .... We will have to grow into a new stage of consciousness to find this undiscovered mental faculty that would empower us with new abilities and intelligence to move our existing strengths beyond the bounds of material limitations extending to a new dimension that shifts the values of our accomplishments beyond its mortal destiny.

I was always curious and fascinated by writings on human potentialities, of powers within and beyond the mind, of paranormal events and also many things of life, that were unexplainable, but still existent ... I'm not a psychologist or a scientist,but driven by the fact that the knowledge about the science of life still remains undiscovered. I wish I had a scientific and logical explanation so unquestionably we could hold hands and walk across the bridge, but instead we stand here in a perceptual threshold knowing well that which is extra-ordinary stands across the river. But we lack the courage to cross. We still remain with an element of doubt that this could be a deception ..and yet we still strive to be extra-ordinary.

The greatest search is to find that which seems invisible, this is what differentiated the great explorers..they were not looking for scientific explanations for everything they set their minds on ... they had the courage to leave the present shore ..they came to terms with these realities ...... We have got to come to terms with what's beyond the horizon without which we would not understand and relate to its environment.

Just as the whole is greater than the sum of its constituent parts ... the integrated power of all our faculties gives rise to another undiscovered, unrecognized faculty which has the ability to empower us to aspire and accomplish extraordinary feats in our life's.

When I speak of our faculties, I'm referring to our faculties that comes into play when pursuing a certain goal in life. Our conscious efforts should be in line with our deep intentions ......

Our unconscious minds should not be an obstruction by way of interference from within.

It is this integration this alignment and convergence that gives rise to a new and adequate cognitive instrument that transforms us to people of a higher order of logics and understanding and an explosion from a five sensory mentally prisoned personality to a multi sensory extraordinary individual.

It is this expanded perceptions and intelligence that enabled the greatest people in this planet to move their work and their professions to a new dimension empowering them to perform at extraordinary levels ... *leaving their names echoing across the planet for many centuries.*

"Leaving your present shore, and striding out into new horizons will get you lonely, segregated, like cast away ...... fears of failure, lack of confidence, discouragement will grip you all the time ...... If you turn back to look with skepticism and doubt ... disastrous forces will wash you back to the same shore.

Despite adversities, If you stand firmly, courageously clinging on to your beliefs and convictions you'll get to where only a few extraordinary individuals will dare.

"We are moving out of The Conventional and old school thoughts, obstinately been bold and daring to explore the invisibilities and conquering the impossibilities of life."

"YOU" In Control

Imagine you are in the control seat of a very powerful Project. Every little participating part in this project is within your control except for one constituent part which plays a Major role in the smooth movement of this project.. What could be the ultimate outcome.?

Its the same logic when we are pursuing astounding, Legendary heights in life. You'll find us ...... on once ... off once ... and even not knowing the reason as to why we drift away from our intended destinations time after time. Many of us become disturbed when we fail in our endeavors to achieve something we set our minds on, so our state of mind is often shaped by failures and successes ...... We are buoyant in fair weather and depressed and despondent in adversity. In short our biological system interacts with our intra-psychic system and with the social systems (friends, relations, organizations family) of which we are all a part.

A burning desire or a thought alone in isolation cannot stimulate action toward a set task and drive this whole mechanism toward that destination ...... We could study deeply each constituent part of our whole biological system, we also could study the psychological aspect of each individual, make observations of any malfunctioning organs, diagnose any disease, take remedial measures, replace major organs, work on therapies ... but we should also know the meaning of this whole mechanism put together. Like the mechanism of the clock whose ultimate outcome is to indicate time so does our whole mechanism working towards a destination a movement to an ultimate result.

This mental instrument is the ultimate power that has control over Body and Mind, a Cognitive instrument that emerges out of the electro magnetic processes of the re-association of all faculties which connects you to your higher self, your higher intelligence, that can maximize your powers of the mind ... and draw powers beyond the mind. This integrated power is your power house that stores the ultimate in human potentialities.

When all your mental domains namely your Conscious Mind, your Unconscious Mind and your Sub-Conscious Mind are working in one direction, it engages your total potentials. There's no ambiguity, no obstruction, there's naked attention in whatever you do. Your cognitive skills are maximized resulting in the emergence of a new cognitive instrument through the partnership and harmony of all your conscious domains moving in one direction to meet your objectives ...... This new cognitive instrument is the flame that lightens our Passions ... retains our determinations to pursue our goals in life.

Let's prepare ourselves to perceive the world with this new light, move our work and life to a new dimension giving us a new vision for a higher destiny in life ...... continuing our success stories beyond materialism ......

leaving our names echoing across the planet for many more centuries to come.

Primarily we should be aroused by intellectual curiosity and intellectual comprehension ... which will take us to actual realization and practice in this interest. We should be ready for boldness and extravagance, despite the hazards that we may face on this journey ...... and this may well give us courage and strength to view the possibilities of moving our professions and our life to a new dimension.

Instead of shutting ourselves from the unknown we should boldly move forward paying attention very strongly and put all our efforts and energies in discovering the unknown than accepting the fact that we are functioning with just only a ten percent of our true potentialities.

SUBMERGING OUR MORTALITY

We long for eternal experiences of success ...... but that fear of the inability to go on and on strikes us like lightning, the skull starring right in our eyes grinning in the banquet ... bringing us down as we try to fight back real hard to imagine live and act like we are immortal.

We spend our entire life consciously or unconsciously trying to deny death ... both by constructing and manipulating a subjective life and by erecting permanent and timeless objects as outward and visible signs of a hope for immortality. We want nothing less than eternal prosperity ...... Right along history man erected cultural symbols which do not age or decay to quiet his fear of his death of his self and his name.

No matter what kind of argument could be brought in here ...... If we had a choice of a device to ensure immortality of our flesh and blood ... its a big YES ...... but in the absence of this power, we settle for our second choice ... by creating Chronicles that would "Assure our names to go on and on into many more centuries to come."

Welcome to A Community of

A few extraordinary Individuals.

PART 11

An Adequate Mental Instrument

We are going pass the bridge between our physical and our non-physical world. The mental structure that connects us to these two worlds is this INTEGRATION ... the integrated power of our total human faculties ... we cannot engage each of these in isolation to the other. On its own each of these faculties are only serving life in half ... causing conflict and paradox.

There is nothing occult or strange in this ... all this is in line with modern Neuro-physiology which has quite clearly demonstrated that the degree of consciousness is always conditioned by the degree to which a given organism has an integrated unity. ... Consciousness in a scientific perspective is to be understood, in its broadest sense as indicating every kind of intelligences and abilities from the most rudimentary forms of inner perceptions to the human phenomena of reflective thought.

Spiritual perfection and material synthesis are constituent parts of one. In other words powers of this integration serves both purposes ... helps and supports us to realize all our life's goals ..be it material or spiritual ... be it accumulation of wealth, the pursuit for Power or Fame or moving to a new dimension in life ... It is when you function from this higher levels of Consciousness that you feel the reality of been a Legend is an absolute possibility. This strange energy that you feel can drive you to any destination of your choice.

Apart from our normal waking consciousness which we may call our rational consciousness, there lie potential forms of consciousness entirely different. We may go through life without knowing their existence; but by engaging yourself in compulsive mental activities. they are there in all their completeness, definite types of mentality which probably somewhere have their field of application and adaptation. It is a part of the cosmic energy force which is beyond the bounds of our five sensory footprint and which is a non-physical reality. Regarding them is a matter of attitude, belief and conviction despite the fact that they cannot furnish formulas. They open up a new region of consciousness and intelligence although they fail to provide a map.

Only a few extraordinary individuals with intentions of legendary accomplishment will traverse this tough mental terrain.

Shifting our life and our Professions to a new dimension requires us to be attitred with An Adequate Mental Instrument that empowers us, inspires and justifies the ecstasies of this migration ... holding on to our visions of moving our accomplishments beyond our death- stained destinies.

BELIEF CRISIS

Belief is the core of every other dynamics that surrounds a Legendary journey in life ... its the beginning and needs to be sustained with its same power to the end of our journey. It's a switch that can empower and dis-empower the rest of our faculties. When we are on a journey without lit up sign- post to guide us along the way ... our only illumination is our belief.

Everyone of us are faced with this crisis in varying degrees ....

Whenever we set our minds on an errand beyond the capacities of our existing competencies and skills ... skepticism creeps in. ... we scout around for information trying to justify the practicality and the reality of reaching our goals ....we go in search of rationalistic logical cover and completely reject anything with ambiguity and paradox.

"DO NOT BE AFRAID OF BEEN A LEGEND."

We have been shaped and fashioned to what we are today by our beliefs and convictions that we gathered along the way from our parents,Mentors environments and other influencers. Our beliefs are based on a static past and holding on to these beliefs destroys the power of our creativity and exploration. The most powerful element of our mental faculty is our creativity. In this sense beliefs based on a static past can be very detrimental ... it can stop further progression and stand as a barrier for new thinking. Innovation and abstract thinking are skills that encompass the present, the now and the future, the rational and the paradox.

We refuse to challenge our beliefs because change by nature is the strongest resistance in humans ... Holding onto static past beliefs could better us in what we do today. ... it can broaden our knowledge ... but it lacks the power to discover new intelligencies and abilities.

It is useful to challenge our own beliefs. Looking for new intelligencies does not leave you with a detailed route map with all sign post on the way ... nor does it give you sufficient data for analysis. It could only give you a glimpse of hope. Our past belief systems should be a contributory factor to our explorations and not an obstacle stopping or slowing down our progress toward moving our life and profession to a new dimension.

Restructuring and creating new beliefs needs an explorative mind and a challenging attitude ... Firstly, you need to re-examine your existing beliefs and overwrite them with your new ones. Some of them you need to wipe-out some of them you need to re-think ... and add on new writings into your belief system ...... Further, you need to move from a close system of thinking to a open system. It is your beliefs that shapes and fashions your personality ... beliefs gives rise to your source traits..or let us say your roots. Affirmations auto suggestions etc. can help if they are performed at the root level. This root level is your innermost self ... the executive chamber of your mind ... where your beliefs are treasured.

Getting to the root of your mind..to the root of your beliefs requires a weeding process. It's the freeing of your mind of all other occupations ... conscious and unconscious. Your mind should be as fresh as an unused hardware system of a powerful computer ... ready to take in some powerful software ... so in fact you need to primarily, de-program your mind.

Trying to battle on the surface with a set of simple practical rules in order to build your new beliefs is like fertilizing a plant along with its weeds ... you'll find yourself in an endless battle within you ... like a charioteer with two head strong horses pulling in two different directions. You'll be like a splintered personality ... on again ... off again..finding it extremely difficult to be on course.

We have been to fiery seminars listened to many on "How to

change" ... At these sessions our beliefs are hyped up immediately..but in no time we find us loosing all that confidence that energy ... the reality of legendary accomplishments seems to move away from us day by day..very soon pushing us back to square one..back in our same boots with the same crowd living this life most tragically like half a human. Changing beliefs is taking a total transformation ... it needs an effort as much as a re-creation of your total self.. like a re-engineering of your mechanism.

There are no sets of habits or step by step rules to follow ... Its your Autonomous choice and will, constructed from the seat of your Mind's Executive Chamber.

You cannot compromise with belief ... either you believe or you don't ... if you move forward without establishing genuine belief you are in fact like a ship without a rudder ... vulnerable to any type of invasions that can drift you off course ... you are wasting your energies and efforts. Belief ...... controls your power of comprehension, your power of engagement your power of direction. To believe in what's extraordinary primarily you need to place yourself above the average person You need to have higher perceptive powers, higher visionary foresight and a sensory capacity that empowers you to feel see and comprehend what others are unable to.

Believing facts beyond scientific acceptance, primarily requires the arousal of your curiosity, the willingness and liberty for hypothesis and extrapolation of matters of life.

We are on an extraordinary journey and do not have any sign post or past statistics to build our confidence that we are in the right direction. Our only supportive armory is our Level of consciousness, an advanced cognitive instrument, and the ability we possess to see the world and perceive it with a higher level of logics and understanding ...... this is our defence in this bold and daring majestic journey ......

Take pleasure ... hold yourself with high Self-Esteem ... Only a few are privileged to be.....

"Recognised as True Legends."

"Aspirations in life takes dramatic changes.

With every stage in growth and development we tend to aspire higher and higher.

The ultimate aspiration in life is to ensure that our accomplishments continues beyond life's mortal boundaries......

"LEAVING BACK OUR NAMES TO GO ON FOREVER."

Elmo Ebert

GUIDE THE WORLD

No matter where in the planet we live … no matter what our origins are … when viewed and perceived from a higher level of logics and understanding, we are people of one planet … people of the same human anatomical conception … people who have the same potentialities to develop themselves to what they want to be.

Today we have created boundaries in habitations …… different Levels in social standings …… recognition linked to wealth and power and many other demographics that has blinded and deceived us from our origins … created unequal opportunity perhaps leaving out the greatest scholars and scientist that never had the chance to serve the world and its people.

A few greats, walk this planet, who never acknowledged, accepted or was influenced by these worldly set norms and standards … but pursued their great aspirations despite adversities … perhaps in pain and tears working tirelessly with utmost belief and confidence in their visions to serve the whole of humanity and ……

"Leaving their names echoing across the planet for many more centuries to come."

WEALTH, POWER & FAME are material possessions that gets completely detached from us along with our mortal destiny. It should be our ultimate quest to engage our strengths and find ways beyond our mortal destinies … to serve the people of this planet … for many more centuries …… not simply a handful of people that we have control of today … but the whole of humanity. The world awaits individuals such as you and I are, to guide them, show them real values and meanings of purposeful living and ways of living their lives in honorability integrity and in truthfulness.

Lets disseminate our knowledge and our intelligence that we have encompassed along the way so that they will reach every corner of this planet serving people without any difference in race colour or any other human assessments ... helping and supporting them to live a fulfilling life.

As we surrender to our mortal destinies ... despite the fact it maybe beyond our powers to sense or see OUR NAMES REMEMBERED BY THE WORLD ...

"let,s be content and feel its glory today and now ... Lets feel the glory the honor and the ecstasy of being an Individual who toils in the mind to righteously, preserve the energy and serenity of this planet and its people not for a few, but for many generations and for many centuries to come."

A DARK AND WINDING ROAD..

There is no easy way to move your work to great levels. If what we have accomplished in life is by following a few simple and practical rules..They don't transform you to be an extraordinary Individual"

You cannot live an ordinary life and then achieve extra ordinary heights in life. ... everyone loves simplicity, practicality when it comes to aspiring and setting goals in life. The truth is Legendary accomplishments have never been simple, didn't seem practical, seemed like irrational illogical. ... even to the extents of looking non-sensical at the beginning of every task toward it.

When moving into unknown terrains ... everything seems fogged with elements of doubt and understanding at the beginning..

On the road to unequaled performances in life you find yourself very lonely, singled out fighting your own battle ...... passionately holding on to that belief that conviction and the confidence ... to retain the reality of your great aspirations in life.

Moving your work to legendary levels involves Pioneering, creating, exploring and the liberty for extrapolations and hypothesis. It requires a daring attitude, an adventurous mind ... and most of all it requires a human instrument that can perceive the world with a higher level of significance .... in the sense that we see not only the physical or the visibility of objects and people but the non-physical and the invisibilities of everything in life and this Universe.

As we cross boundaries of our existing knowledge and in-telligence ... we move away from simplicity we move away from what seemed practical, logical rational ... we move into a more complex world ...... a world perceived with a higher level of consciousness ...... this is the exploration into the unknown, this is the favorite playing field of great minds. It is only from this Arena that the greatest people walked this planet and so the world still "Remembers their Name"

The knowledge the intelligence the skills and competencies to survive and win in this arena lies within the greatest Academy that we have been gifted with ... but remains beyond our ordinary visions and comprehension ... and this academy is deep within you. Enrollment to this Academy is with no-charge ... eligibility are your attitudes,your beliefs, convictions and self-confidence. This I may say is the most highest and complex test an individual could ever face.

The maps of real knowledge and intelligence designed for Legendary accomplishments are stored deep within this Mysterious Academy.

There are many who have very successfully applied various simple practical ways of attracting Power, Wealth and Fame ... but there are only a few extra-ordinary individuals who had accomplished ... that which cannot be equaled by another. Sometime in history, we needed muscle to be ahead in our environments, which then gave way for muscle and mind ... today we have arrived at a time when we require a human instrument beyond the capacities of our mind and our physical senses in order to confront these dramatically changing Political, Social and economic challenges.

With this huge acceleration in the rate of growth of facts, of knowledge and technical advancement it seems so obvious that today, we need a different kind of a human-being with a change of attitude and disposition ...... an individual that can perceive the world with mysterious foresight who can confront any challenges in the absence of forewarning.

There were a few on board this Historic Universal vessel who saw things beyond the capacities of their physical senses and gave us extra-ordinary insights to build richer and richer environments to live a great life-style that we do today ...... there were the others who used this extra-ordinary visions and foreknowledge to guide us toward the ultimate in self-actualization and enlightenment in a spiritual sense ... These great people that walked this planet had the same source of energy and higher intelligence.. however using them in two different directions ...

"SOME OF THEM USED IT TO ATTRACT POWER WEALTH AND FAME ... AND SOME OF THEM USED IT FOR SPIRITUAL ATTAINMENT. BE IT SPIRITUAL OR MATERIAL IT IS THE SAME POWER THAT CAN TAKE US THERE ... THE DIFFERENCE IS YOUR AUTONOMOUS CHOICE."

In Pursuit Of A Legacy

Religions and religious teachings have transformed people,s life's into the better. Certain Philosphies of good living have changed people's life into the positive in attitudes and a way of life ... Great thought Leaders have inculcated these values among the masses dessiminating their intelligence and knowledge and serving the children of the planet not for a day not for a generation but for many years and many more generations to come leaving back their names echoing across the planet .... moving their values beyond mortal boundaries.

Knowledge about the physical universe is made known to us through scientific, astrophysical and other relevant disciplines. We live only by the facts known to us,content with the limited knowledge and stressfully stretching out ourselves for greatness with these limitations.

Every second all over the world thousands of experts and Companies are working hard writing software for business efficiencies systems and procedures. What about the Human Mind ? ....its potentialities ... what about the unknowns.? Each time we sparked with new discoveries about our true potentialities ...... we are compelled to fall back in the absence of scientific facts ....believing that it is only that's visible and factual, as the only available source to move forward.

One time the world never believed or saw anything beyond the capacity of the naked eye..until the microscope unveiled to us a whole new world.

With what ignorance have we been living in the past.!

In the absence of an instrument to capture the invisibilities of life and the universe ... are we to say that it is beyond the scope of human comprehension..or instead discover an instrument that will enable us to see the invisible.?

New ideas are produced through the analysis of data coming through our sensory system. But the significance of the data you receive will depend on the mental state of perception.

So one might perceive the physical world as it appears and form all his ideas accordingly. But one with a higher level of perception will comprehend the physical world with its true meaning ...... example one may form ideas of the planets the sun and planetary movements as they appear and simply as a part of this gigantic universe..but another will perceive these movements as having a significant influence on human affairs here on earth.

To see things beyond its physical appearances we need to first create these possibilities, speculations, and hypotheses and construct them in the executive chamber of our minds.

We are all excellent at adaptation. Our brains all the time seeks to adapt to and learn about the world as it is. In this comfort zone, how could it adapt to a future world.? How could it ..originate.. create?

In this comfort zones we get only better and better in what we do..but it takes us lesser and lesser in our power to create.

"REFUSING TO SEE POSSIBILITIES IN LIFE IS AN EXTREME STAGE OF BLINDNESS ......

Discovering what isn't visible and incomprehensible is the greatest search."

Our personal comfort zone ...... this is where most want to be. By nature one of our rigid stands is to be where we are securing ourselves ...... most look for comfort irrespective of the fact whether they may not contribute toward our growth and development. Clinging to comfort zones is an obsession. If you dont take courage to leave the present shore ... you really shut yourself from a world of possibilities, shut yourself from moving your work to a new dimension.

Most Legends acted on their impulse and instincts and were driven by inner satisfaction rather than worldly achievement. Although by professional demands or other they had to indulge themselves in the tangible world..they had strong attunement to the intangible..to the indefinable. Their drives and ambitions were powered by their mystical and intuitive sensitivity ... intuitional promptings gave them that extraordinary insight to many goals that they set in life. These great people have had many unusual and unexplainable experiences, which are beyond the comprehension of the rational mind.

Real true facts about life were unveiled to us by only a few individuals right along the way. The rest of the world were observant's and followers.

Its time we lead the change ... to lead the change we need a restructuring of our beliefs and convictions ...... change our attitudes and compulsively look for cognitive instruments that will differentiate us from the rest in terms of intelligencies and abilities.

You certainly become better and better in what you do from time to time within your boundaries of skills and competencies, acquiring wealth power or fame. But the pursuit for legendary accomplishments, leading the world to friendlier better and richer environments requires a cognitive shift in your pragmatic thinking, your disposition your attitudes and the way you move forward.

As you undo your skeptic armory attiring yourself with an Adequate mental instrument to migrate to a new dimension, it is of supreme interest that you engage yourself in positive compulsive mental activities regularly to protect you from negative intrusions that can invade you from the outside world via your physical sensory channels, as well as your mental domains such as your unconscious and your subconscious minds.

It is inevitable that many contradictory views and negative

thoughts will stand as obstructions in this journey not accepting these highly unconventional and perhaps controversial thoughts and views of living a life that gives you an undying recognition beyond mortal limitations. Many questions crosses your mind aggressively in debate of this quantum shift and by nature supporting you to remain where you are in this comfort zone.

No surprise, it was so with most all great legends who changed this world to the better ...... and as we know, only a few extraordinary people could have gone through these mental conflicts and adversities that kept bringing down their confidence again and again.

> Just as you are ...... a very few individuals are privileged with extraordinary intelligence, abilities and the required attitudes to move to astounding heights in life .... In this perspective, giving this greatness an undying recognition is a graceful effort.

Elmo Quotes.

SHIFTING your thinking your perceptions and your work to a new dimension can be perceived in different levels of significance and can also be highly contested and personalized. It can be relevant to a particular person, object or place.

A legendary accomplishment to us is a reality when we transform ourselves to be Extra-ordinary individuals connected with our higher intelligence ... helping and supporting people to accomplish their worldly or spiritual goals.

A legacy will loose its glory if what has been achieved can be equaled by each and every individual. ... your name will only be remembered among the list of legends ... if what you do or achieve in life is beyond the capacities of an ordinary individuals reach.

Most times we hit ourselves against a barrier in our progression toward exploring our true possibilities. Sometimes the very idea of being a Legend brings fear to us just like our weaknesses do … and our potentialities lies unused and under-developed. We see ourselves as a true legend only at moments of courage and confidence we only visualize our highest possibilities at these glorious times and are thrilled with them. … but at adverse conditions we recoil in fear before these same possibilities. Most times we are ambivalent and in perpetual conflict about our own highest possibilities.

The pursuit of moving life to a new dimension interms of consciousness,intelligence and abilities is only a passion of a few extra-ordinary people.

These People who are moved by …………

- *An inexpressible dedication and commitment toward achieving what seem an impossibility …… irrespective of the fact whether they are of a material or spiritual nature.*

- *People not looking back, working untiringly with consistency and enthusiasm to find the slightest indication that will lead them to new discoveries in human possibilities ….*

- *People who develop a stable mind-set giving them the power to accept the fact that legendary accomplishments is within their reach..*

- *People who will build an indomitable mental mechanism to sustain and retain this passion and positive state of mind to get there …*

- *People who will see themselves ecstatic at the summit of success supported by their vivid imaginations..*

- *People who drive themselves skillfully toward their destinations with strong belief and confidence in what they do …*

- *People who will use adversities to their advantage to discover and experience their true genius in all circumstances.*

- *People who are bold and daring and will use their liberty to extrapolate and project themselves at that glorious moment of greatness.*

"You have been shaped and fashioned to what you are today as a prestigious individual, by your own beliefs and value systems that you have inherited and embraced along the way ...

Your world of tomorrow will be designed and created by your own mental architecture of life."

Elmo Ebert.

THE BEST PLACE TO BEGIN

Every majestic tree that grows to giant out in the wilderness has its concept rapped in its roots. despite any obstruction it may face in its growth process it will ultimately shape and fashion itself to maintain its originality ...

We are the ultimate creation in natures wondrous life forms ... we are positive by origin ... and great by nature. Winds of disaster have swept across the landscape of our greatness, with life's eventualities, clouding the illumination that brightens us from deep within our inner-most self..

All we need to do is ...

RE-CONSTRUCT OUR ORIGINALITY ... sweep away the debris to encompass and experience our Greatness.

There are two ways in attempting to get to our destination. You can get there step by step as if climbing up a ladder tightening each rung as you go by. Here in the process of clinging on to these rungs you loose your freedom ... your freedom to extrapolate ....for hypothesis ... to adventure ... explore ... to visualize and discover many other ways of ascending there.

The other is to virtually be up there with the power of your Intentions, your Vivid imaginations and the power to create this reality in your mind. From this elevated point you pull yourself up there with consistent compulsive mental activities relevant to your task.

- *Exercise your liberty to hold you in high -Esteem beyond the glories of Power, Wealth & Fame*
- *Boldly accept the fact that you are empowered with this extraordinary intelligence and abilities to place yourself above others.*

- *That you can sense feel and reach heights that only a few will dare.*
- *You will not see yourself in that dimension unless your minds-eye is presently equipped with an instrument that can visualize you there.*
- *You can only create a great future ..if you have the correct disposition to create a great now ....*
- *Your mind will not produce thoughts of a legendary nature unless it is attuned to an appropriate channel that elicits legendary aspirations.*

Your mission should be to take a quantum leap today into an environment that legends inhabit ... sights sounds feelings they are all directed toward moving your life to that dimension that empowers you to bring about a total transformation from a power or wealth driven life to an individual that can guide the world to a more purposeful and meaningful living ...... that will hold your achievements with an undying recognition ... *"leaving your name back echoing across the planet for many more centuries to come."*

"Nothing can be AUTHENTICALLY sensed ... seeing or experienced without an adequate mental instrument of perception and understanding."

If right at the beginning of this magnificient journey you neglect or restrict the use of your faculties of cognition..it will inevitably bring down your levels of aspirations..you will see the world less meaningful lesser rich in opportunities and disinteresting than it actually is. Attiring yourself with the required mental gear right at the beginning of this journey enables you to awaken your dormant faculties of cognition to discover new meanings,new riches and new interest ..that seemed inaccessible to you earlier.

"GRACIOUSLY DIFFERENT"

"In order to move to a higher level of consciousness..it is categorical that we shift from OUR PRESENT state of cognition to a state of meta-cognition ... thinking about our thinking and challenging our own pragmatic analysis and conclusive decisions"

Great journeys began with great mind-sets ...... mind-sets that were created by viewing and comprehending the world with a higher level of significance.. We should Develop this through the liberty and the power we possess to nurture our minds to create it.

Just like a racing champ understands the capacity of his machine..without which he is unable to drive it with its maximum power ... so should we primarily have this power of perception to comprehend life in its fullest form engage and actualize its total potential.

Unlike plants and animals we have something more of a mysterious nature ... a mysterious power ... we are of a higher power than consciousness ...... we are not mere thinkers but thinkers capable of observing our own thinking ...... capturing intelligence beyond the bounds of our five sensory footprint that connects us to our higher Intelligent faculty.

This power opens us up to a world of possibilities.

Biological changes took place in many to bring along many kinds of species in life forms to ultimately take form of this most complexed and paradoxical Human- being as we are today .... These biological changes resulted in neurological development giving rise to our brains to grow us and move us from one stage to another stage of consciousness ... from a state of a subconscious to a semi-conscious and to a self conscious stage that we are today ... the growth continues.. There is no reason to believe that it has saturated.

We live with the belief that the only source of data that comes to us is via our five senses and that a data processing unit called the brain takes care of all this. These beliefs are restricting us from discovering other instruments of cognition, narrowing down the true realities of our world. The advancement in science and technology and a mechanized, automatized living style have further restricted the use of the human instrument of cognition, in a somewhat extreme way.

These advancements in science and technology could only give us better and richer environments, but will not contribute toward the progress of our cognitive powers or the discovery of new intelligence, helping us to perceive the world with a higher level of significance.

The power to move your life and work to a new dimension needs to be primarily created in the workshop of your mind ...... created in its real sense before it can be actualized..This brings us to the point where we should comprehend our senses, our abilities our powers of cognition in its true fullness ... without which we will perceive the world and its possibilities inadequately.

The fundamental problem of most many living with this deception, that moving their Professsions and life to a new dimension is beyond their reach ... is due to the lack of real knowledge of one's total concept as a human species and one's ignorance of their true potentialities.This creation is not a simple playful imagination, visualization or a thought. It has to originate not in your ordinary mind ... but through the convergence and unification of all your mental faculties..or with this new cognitive instrument that emerges with this integration.

The mind is an ever developing ever evolving entity which still remains undiscovered in terms of identification and potentialities. Along with our growth in Biological complexities and neurological refinement (especially of our brains) we grow in intelligencies and abilities, this is a developing mind.

Besides this progression of the mind, we as a human species continues to evolve, like in the past resulting in our minds poignant from one stage of consciousness to another.

So we have the mind progressing in two ways;

1. *Developing along with knowledge and experience along the horizontal axis as a constituent part of our neurological and biological growth and development.*

2. *Evolving to higher stages of consciousness vertically, as a human species, in this whole evolutionary process.*

We have no Authority or power to accelerate the growth of our physical bodies or we may say our biological mechanism.But we do have the privilege,the liberty, the power to grow our minds to higher levels of logic and understanding .... in other words..to the Executive Chamber of or Minds.

"Reaching legendary heights in life requires a mental stature that is of an Audacious Nature ... These astounding aspirations often deteriorates in confidence and hope to individuals with a common order of mind .... Only a few extraordinary individuals are privileged to hold-on to realize these majestic accomplishments."

As we move from stage to another stage in Biological complexities, our neurological system too advances from a disarranged to an arrange from a crude to a more refined. Consciousness and Biological complexities are counterparts in the growth and development process of an individual they are interdependent for effective functionalities.

We have got the liberty,the power to race our minds ahead of this combination.

Just like an olympic athlete racing his body to the finishing line engaging all his physical powers ... so should we with our autonomous will engage ourselves in compulsive mental activities ... racing our minds well ahead of its natural growth process. Our minds haven't saturated ... history is still taking us forward. What has really taken place is that we have engaged our minds to give us better and better environments ... and taking us away from where it was meant to grow.

"MINDS HAVE NOT SATURATED ... WE HAVE NOT YET FULLY TRIED THEM"

You can create an adequate Mental instrument to perceive the world and function at a higher level of logic and understanding only if this instrument is architectured and engineered by the integration of all your mental faculties.

Just as a spacecraft requires an adequate flight mechanism to

journey outside the planet to a new dimension in flight experience ... so do we require this adequate mental instrument to journey
outside our five sensory system to a multi-sensory ... from our physical realities to non-physical realities which empowers us to aspire and
accomplish legendary heights that will bring about immense value
to the whole of mankind, *"Holding our great achievements with an
undying recognition and leaving our names back in the planet for many
more centuries to come beyond our mortal destinies."*
**So how do attire ourselves with this Adequate Mental
Instrument.?**

Meditation ... most everybody would agree. But lets look at
the real purpose of meditation first. Meditation is primarily meant
for spiritual purposes..attempting to release your mind from all
sensory input which will enable you to transcend to a higher level of
consciousness at which point you are able to perceive the gateway to
spirituality which appears to you in different forms. The intention
the purpose here is transcendence to a higher plane. This too takes
place when you have reached the executive chamber of your mind.
The difference here is governed by what intentions choice and will
drives you to that point.

We don't need to go through this meditative process, shutting ourselves from our surroundings. We keep our conscious mind
widely open ... functioning .... but we ensure that our unconscious
minds are in partnership with all our endeavours in life.

Mental images..imaginations visualizations will only remain
unrealized ..if they are not created with the integration of all your
mental domains.

Acknowledging this reality, mapping out a process to create this
cognitive instrument should be our quest in life. We should push
boundaries to discover new horizons in mind –power. Doing this
needs a daring exploration into the depths of our mental domain.

"We choose to be great not because the road to greatness is a simple step by step process ... but because it needs to drop an immeasurable amount of sweat ...... in mind and body."

Elmo Quotes

WATCH YOUR MIND

`Our minds when viewed from an higher state of consciousness seems to be like a ship without a rudder finding it extremely impossible to hold on to one direction even on a calm day. When the storm is on, it sways as if to throw itself overboard.

Can we depend on our unprotected minds to guide us along the tuff terrains of life ... or should we not attire it with the required armory that can defend itself from any negative element that can distort our direction in life.

There is a more serious question that remains unanswered ...... Can we engage an unstable,vulnerable mind to attire and control the same mind.?

Or do we have to look beyond its boundaries for a higher mental faculty ?

"As we reach astounding heights in life acquiring Power Wealth and control over our environments … this desire for more and more of Power, accumulation of wealth and controllability grows within us aggressively. This yearning extends to an obsession by our ego -centric attitudes that obstructs us been engaged in any Humanitarian thoughts and activities that's not simply a charitable deed …… but an Innovative thought and a great humanitarian movement that can change the lives of many underprivileged in terms of purposeful and meaningful living.

Elmo Qu*otes*

Exploring beyond your five sensory footprint and moving to a new dimension takes you to alien territory in terms of your thinking, your behavior and aspirations in life.

As you function in this new domain you should be completely liberalized from any negative intrusions. Momentarily, detaching yourself from your past and present in terms of financial or social standings becomes a categorical imperative.

The greatest mental attire to be engaged in humanitarian thoughts and actions is Humbleness.

An Autonomous Choice

Your new intentions of been a humanitarian Legend should be backed by an Autonomous choice and deep intentions. This creation is not an ordinary mental picture that could appear and disappear from your conscious mind with changing environments and circumstances..its a creation that's engraved beyond the capacities of the mind, engraved and depicted deep in your inner self, it is protected by your Autonomous choice and will. ... and backed by your deep intentions.

We need to re-construct ourselves completely..its like clearing the go downs with its old stocks. This process invariably becomes automated,when your new intentions,choices and will are directed toward the greatness you desire to create.

The energy that emanate from your autonomous choice and will is of such a powerful nature that it can gradually eliminate the negatives that lay deep within you..its like you are creating a software program with a dual function of running a new program and at the same time deleting an already existing program. In this process all your efforts and your energies should be focused in your new program empowering it to take control of your total life. This force should be as close as to that of a kind of obsession or addiction transforming your whole metabolism, neurologically and mentally ... as is a team of experts working toward engineering the construction of your new life.

"THIS IS A REAL TRANSFORMATION ... A REAL ARCHITECTURE OF YOUR LIFE'S NEW DESIGN..THIS IS AN AUTONOMOUS CHOICE ... A SELF-GOVERNING WILL ... AND A SOVEREIGN INTENTION."

You live with this every moment of your life.

In life we have made countless number of choices … some of them really contributed toward our personal growth and development..some of them were the wrong ones that in adversity obstructed our progress. Most of these choices weren't autonomous, but were dependent by many who had influence and control over us. We have been gifted with one of the greatest powerful tools in life which is the Liberty and autonomy of choice … the freedom to architect our future.

Lets exercise our freedom righteously and make this autonomous choice of moving our life to a new dimension … and. not let our life's be driven by circumstances …… So lets wake up to be powered by a new energy that drives us across the bridge.

Imaginations of the world you intend creating for yourself means nothing if its not accompanied with your belief and trust in yourself. When it comes to creating your world … you need to take imaginations very seriously ……. to the extend that you mindfully prepare yourself before you engage in these vivid imaginations … when I say "mindfully prepare yourself" what I really mean is liberalizing your mind from any type of intrusions.

It is with this Autonomous choice, will and vivid imaginations connected with your ardent desires and your fierce enthusiastic conscious efforts to get there that primarily transforms mental creations into subtle experiences … and with these repeated experiences … eventually everything turns into a reality.

> "Today the world is at a threshold that will lead to a new horizon in consciousness, intelligencies and abilities … Only a few extra-ordinary minds will have the courage to leave the present shore to perceive the world with this higher level of logics and understanding".

> *ELMO EBERT*

MENTAL CREATIONS & INTENTIONS

The most chaotic board-room sessions takes place in the workshop of our minds ... there is no heirachical structure ... everybody is the boss ... everybody wants to get his thing done .... there's only one way to stop this pandemonium ....

Work as an integrated entity ... inter-dependent ... inter-connected ... moving in partnership and harmony in one direction ...... intentions ... imaginations visualizations thought forces are all aligned looking at the same destination.

Mental creations such as imaginations visualizations transforms into reality when they are in line with your deep intentions. For example you may spontaneously imagine and visualize yourself been awarded one of the most prestigious Global awards for an outstanding humanitarian movement or Business Excellence. If your existing intentions are not in line with these new imaginations ...... they will simply appear and disappear in a short time. If these new visualizations are connected to your intentions they will remain in you deep within upto the point of seen you there in reality.

With a burning desire, like a prayer you need to affirm this to yourself each day, time after time.

The quest for revolutionizing your work should be driven by an irresistible impulse to move forward, minute by minute hour by hour day by day pushing boundaries overcoming adversities ... destroying obstacles to get there.

Look at us through an evolutionary perspective.. .... As a human species we have arrived to the highest point in the organic scale(which is a fully developed neuro system, especially, the Brain) And we now await an elevation to a higher state of consciousness …… and a glimpse even into a world that's beyond the world we know of …… We are not Scientist or philosophers, we are explorers of true human potentialities, and as explorers we will embrace all disciplines that play a role in our ultimate quest to move our life beyond the bounds of our five sensory footprint

And "Only a Few Extra-Ordinary People are Privileged.

When we function at this higher levels of intelligence reaching astounding heights beyond WEALTH. … POWER … AND FAME or reaching any of our life's destinations,becomes a true reality … success becomes inevitable, irrespective of the fact whether they are material or spiritual goals.

Imagine you were a kind of an Artificial intelligence or a programmable Machine..you have got the capacity and power to program your future and all you have to do is just create and click …… Our mission is the same …. we are in search of this password..that gives us access to this power of creating our own program..and we know that this password is treasured within us.

Accomplishing Legendary heights in anything you pursue in life will depend very strongly on …

THE MENTAL-FOUNDATION THAT YOU HAVE LAID.

Just like a high rise building needs a foundation to support that great structure and an architecture which is of the highest standards and ready resources to erect the sky riser. so does greatness that needs a great foundation.

Our First structure is our FOUNDATION … Which ..is our DEEP INTENTIONS created by our Autonomous choice and will.

…

Life's realities remains incomprehensible today ...
fogged and mystified by our dull faculties ... but
as we journey ahead to higher levels of consciousness ... We blow away the haze crystallizing our
visions to sense, see and realize the full potentials
of life.

ELMO EBERT

LEGENDARY ASPIRATIONS

Perhaps you are contemplating on creating a New Philosophy on living a Fulfilled life or on Self-Actualization ... you may want to bring about "Eqality" in social standings among the whole human race ... possibly, to irradicate poverty ... bring about a "Classless Society." Advocate absolute Political Friendship among all nations ... ENSURING THAT ALL NATIONS ARE ABSOLUTELY UNITED WORKING TOWARDS PEACE AND PROSPERITY ... Encourage Great respect and understandings among all religious divisions. ONE GOD ... ONE BELIEF.

Whatever your legendary aspirations are ... its directed towards changing the whole world to a better place to live for everyone ...... not just a few with high social standing, a particular nation or a small community of people.

Legendary accomplishments most times realizes its goals many years after, beyond the mortal destiny of its Initiator ... it broadens in belief and strengths from decade to decade, to ultimately remain an undying Philosophy or noble deed for many centuries to come.

We undergo physical agonies as well as mental,psychological agonies of which the latter is more devastating than the other. No matter what you are, a beggar on the street in an underdeveloped country, or a Billionnaire in the most sophisticated city ... agonies don't vary in pain along with social or financial status. You don't have to be a billionaire or a celebrity to bring solace to another distressed Billionnaire or to a Powerful Political Leader or celebrity ...... you can tranquilize their trauma with a few words of your wisdom and high intelligence.

Many facts seem abstract and incomprehensible today when viewed with our dull minds ... but as the world evolve from one stage to another in consciousness and intelligence we sense, see and capture the world with a higher level of logics and understanding empowering us to aspire and reach legendary heights in life.

Its not POWER,WEALTH or FAME that makes you a "True Legend" but your automomous will and your humanitarian inclination to bring solace and value in every aspect to the people of the planet.

A Vivid Imagination

Vividly Imagine yourself well above an average individual, above your colleagues, friends and relatives and other influencers. Remember ...... don't involve your Ego-Mind in this exercise,which means you are not trying to place yourself above others in relation to POWER ... WEALTH OR FAME ... but in your levels of consciousness ... in other words you place yourself as a more evolved person than the rest of them.

In this imaginative mental activity Let there be no interference whatsoever from your Ego Mind. Drop your self-crowned deceptive attitude ... you are about to put on a new extraordinary mental device.

FOR NOW ... VISUALIZE YOURSELF ...... as that extra-ordinary individual ... its like you are looking down at every other thing from an higher elevation ... silence your logical mind ... let yourself be driven by that inexpressible feeling that erupts from within you ... let that sensation persist ..let your heart take-over .... engage your emotions ... your feelings ....

NOW ...... "VISUALIZE A NEW 'YOU'" ..this is an ego-drive free exercise ... place yourself at a higher Level of logics and understanding ...... put on this extra mental/cognitive device that helps and supports you to perceive the world differently than the rest of them. Let's be real here ... you will lose it many times ... but the key point here is that each time you lose it, you need to aggressively re-create it.

You are in fact developing a new mental habit, and just as the growth of an individual it has its stages of growth ... from an infant right upto a matured individual. This new mental exercise will also inevitably go through its development stage, missing focus and direction several times ... unable to hold-on to any kind of support or move in progression ... but by and by it stays steady institutionalized into you ... let your belief be your mentor and director in this exercise.

Remember higher levels of consciousness is not gained by an academic qualification Power or wealth ... it is a natural evolvement ... and this process can be brought under your governance only through compulsive mental engagement, which means that it is required of you to repeat this exercise several times a day until such time it transforms to an automated process within you..eventually your beliefs and convictions in yourself as a higher person in intelligencies and abilities gets engraved within you empowering you with an adequate cognitive instrument to perceive and perform to reach beyond the limits of an ordinary mind ... migrating your life and your profession to a new dimension .... standing on new ground contemplating of bringing positive change not simply to a group of people around you but to the whole of the human race for many more centuries to come.

Its not about how much your money can buy ... how much your power can control or how recognized you are.? ...... Its about how evolved you are above others ... how high you stand in levels of consciousness, intelligencies and abilities ..its about the power you have acquired to move your work and your life to a new dimension where only a few extraordinary can be.

Its about how you shine out ... resounding a vibrance that emanates from you that can be sensed and seeing by the world.

You and I are different, and what makes us different is our great attitudes and bold and confident approach toward life. We are POSITIVE BY ORIGIN, each one of us has the same foundation on which greatness can be build ...... but we keep losing our positive originality in this world that's dominated by negative irrational energies.

If you deeply analyze the disturbances caused to your life especially those of a psychological nature ... you'll note that a good part of it erupts from your ego-mind ...... your ego-mind is a separate mental entity ...... created by you ... yes it does drive you to aspire higher and higher in life ... but you need it only to the extend that it does not stand as an obstruction in your decision making process ... your ego mind can come in as a suppportive motivator to aspire higher in life but not as a supportive decision maker dressed with its upright attitude that can distort the good decision making process ...... this consciousness this observation is of paramount importance if we are to move our life's to a new dimension.

Once the ego emerges it can repress and distrort your valuable source traits which in turn can also change your surface traits ... and in fact these distortions can boomerang back to the ego ... so you'll go through life with a crippled ego, which can be detrimental and obstructive in terms of your growth and development.

THE PRIMARY STRUCTURE ...
OUR FOUNDATION

Life is dramatized by agonies and ecstasies ... success and failure all the time. Some of them comes into play by choice and some by circumstances.

But let us agree on this one..Living our life is certainly by choice.. Architecturing and engineering our future is certainly by choice.

We have got all the liberty to choose the way you want your life to move ahead. Despite the fact that you may face adversities along the way, you got the liberty and the power to be on course, to reach your intended destination.

You can feel the glory and ecstasy of success in two different ways:

One: You can choose and strive to be the best among the ..ORDINARY working within the capacities of your physical –mind.

TWO:..You can choose to be. EXTRA-ORDINARY ...... encompassing your non-physical realities ... In the sense that you have moved to a new dimension in your work and life carrying the glory of your efforts and energies beyond mortal boundaries.

In the ordinary Arena ...... you are battling to be the best with the limited weaponry that is known and available to you today and as at now ... you are aggressively in pursuit of Power,Wealth & Fame.

In the extra-ordinary ..your weaponry is of a superior nature ... capturing data from a wider dynamical zone which is unknown and inaccessible to AN ORDINARY MIND ... and this makes you ... ".INTELLECTUALLY LEGENDARY"

You have been given one of the greatest gifts in life ... THE AUTONOMY OF CHOICE AND WILL ... with which you have the power to architect your life and build your own future. However, there is something of paramount importance that should be noted here ... If you don't have that Executive Authority over your thoughts and actions .... you cannot exercise your choice or will .... your journey would be like a ship without a rudder. Carried away by the forces of nature away from your destination of life.

We need to be conscious about our total metabolism and the dynamics around our life, so that we may take complete control of it.

"LETS EXERCISE OUR CHOICE AND HAVE CONTROL OVER IT, AND NOT LET OUR LIFE BE DRIVEN BY CIRCUMSTANCES"

Each time you pick-up a book that's directed towards helping and supporting you to understand the science of Successfull living, ... just stop to think for a while ... ask yourself if the last one really contributed towards your personal development. ... You will find it extremely difficult to answer that one, because whatever development that has taken place in you, seems to have come, mostly, from your own self –directed attitude and drives ...... certainly they were very inspiring, motivational, knowledgeable, ... and they certainly created an instant "Positive state of Mind" and you did get back value for your investment of time and money .... But there was something really missing ...... They failed to keep you sustaining to that positive state of mind retaining that passionate drive for greatness, holding on to those breakthrough concepts. And by and by that flame which suddenly gave light to your life began to lose its illumination quietly pushing you back into darkness once again .... perhaps, this drama went on for many years. ... on again.. off again. you are up once ... down again ...... Negative elements kept invading your mind all the time..you had no control to stop these invasions..although you were consciously battling to be on course, winds of disaster kept blowing viciously against you.

Today you have exercised your autonomous choice and will. Today you have set your mind to move to a new dimension … that's an accomplishment. now you need to protect that mind-set. You need a stronger mental weaponry to lay an indomitable foundation. So your real foundation are your. **DEEP** intentions created by your AUTONOMOUS CHOICE AND WILL.

Intentions are like the backstage supportive mechanism of a drama ……….

"HOWEVER MUCH THE HERO PLAYS HIS ROLE ON THE FRONT STAGE … IF IT IS NOT IN RELATION TO THE BACKSTAGE MECHANISM, THE HERO WILL LOOK LIKE A CLOWN IN THE EYES OF THE AUDIENCE."

SO ..WHAT REALLY IS AN INTENTION.

An intention is not only what you mean or you represent, or you stand for. It is also your beliefs … your desires..and also your perceptions …… So with every changing intention … your thought forces change..your beliefs change and your perceptions change in other words it is your intentions that drives you …. this drive is an AUTOMATED process … If your conscious efforts in life are not in line with your intentions then although you maybe consciously driving in a certain direction … your intentions are pulling you in a different direction. Take an example …… If your deep intentions were to look for unethical, dishonorable ways of attracting power wealth and fame, then however much consciously you battle to work with integrity … you find yourself losing out in all your efforts to get to your destination … *"Righteously."*

Here there is conflicting interest between your conscious mind and your unconscious mind. They are not aligned, not in harmony.. not moving together in the right direction … this conflict disassociates your Mental faculties … disassociates your body and mind, this is not strange, it is common among ordinary people. This is certainly the very reason that everyone cannot perform at astoundingly high levels in whatever they do.

When all our mental faculties are integrated .. ... your Intentions, Conscious Mind, and Unconscious mind it sparks out giving out an illumination, a magical mental device that empowers you to function at your best ... at your maximum potential, intelligencies and abilities ... this is your new COGNITIVE INSTRUMENT. The controlling switch to turn it on is in your custody ... beliefs, convictions, awareness, a higher state of logics and understanding, the correct disposition, the correct attitude and more, are the elements that constitutes the device to open the gate to this extraordinary power. Here you are connected to your higher intelligencies, you,ll amazingly find yourself at your best and even struck by wonder at your capabilities. It is as if three powerful energy sources are wired into one ... to generate maximum energy to support a giant project.

So primarily it is of utmost importance that we examine our intentions which remains partly in our unconscious mind and time after time moves to our conscious minds depending on circumstance and situations.

Use the power of your "AUTONOMOUS WILL & CHOICE" Empower yourself to make a Resolution that is built on a rock-foundation.

- *Ground an indomitable and spirited foundation.*
- *Hold on to your convictions despite adversities*
- *Accept the fact that beginnings will not be perfect ... conceding and moving forward is a perfect beginning.*

Your intentions create the reality that you experience. Until you become aware of this, it happens unconsciously. Therefore be mindful of what you intend. This is the first step in ensuring that you are moving in the correct direction in life. If this foundation is of a substandard quality, your entire life's sky riser can collapse.

The more we rise up in power,wealth and fame the stronger is our desire to go on … and … on.

In the absence of this power we are left with just one choice …

To leave back our names echoing across the planet for many more centuries to come." *Elmo*

Negative influencers will always appear and disappear ... attempting to obstruct this majestic journey. The more you are supportive of this influence the more will you turnaround from this journey.

One such powerful element is your Ego - Mind supporting to create non-realistic Intellects situationally that can be detrimental when an individual is attempting to progress in a particular direction or make an Authentic decision that can make a positive transformation in life.

Decisions made through the influence of your Super egos are altogether not misleading ... however in failing to engage your total self it cuts you away from realizing your full mental potentials in arriving at decisions. You are functioning dis-integrated from your higher intelligencies, from your true Greatness" or your Executive mind .... where the real "YOU" dwells.

Super ego influenced decisions are very close to perfection comparatively with your desired end result.

The point here is ...... how desirable is your end result in view of your own or the growth of your organization? Is this result originating only through the energies of a single constituent part of your system? Will this particular result positively contribute towards your overall success in life?

As an example, is that decision made just to ensure that you maintain your self esteem.? Or in the process are you shutting yourself from many opportunities that can make a positive significant change in your life that would take you to legendary accomplishments in life.

When we have reached this super ego state of mind it is absolutely difficult to change our thinking. The ego is so stable, so permanent, so strong that we tend to deny any separation, stubbornly holding on to our beliefs and convictions. We begin to form a conception of ourselves as static, permanent and this thought chains us from exploring ourselves further.

We should protect ourselves from being intellectually immature and not create these rigid entities that stand as obstructions or mental blocks on our way to progression.

With the growth of our mental-egoic structures come along destructive and evil activities that contaminate our professions. With the ego level we reach a stage that our separate self is so complex and so strong that it could very stubbornly refuse cooperation with the rest of our faculties. It works in isolation denying its independence on the rest of our faculties. It rises up in arrogance and violence to prove its innocence.

We have experienced this in our day to day life. There may have been many instances where we have lost opportunity in life … with our egoic mentalities aggressively holding on to its independence … which we wrongly interpret as our beliefs, values and convictions … ignorant of the fact that some of these beliefs and values have been created by the demands of our super egos that dominate our true life.

NOTE

As I'm addressing my views to a few extraordinary Individuals ... my approach is a self directive exercise and not a conventional step by step progressive methodology.

This self directed progress should find you moving upward driven by your own convictions, from that initial stages of fascination and curiosity to comprehend and believe ... leading to actual practice in moving your life to a new dimension connecting you to your higher -mental faculties, to your higher self, empowering you with new intelligence and abilities ...

"supporting you to Intend, Imagine,visualize, affirm, think and live like a legend."

A philosophy of any nature can only leave you with guidance and with a deep thought provoking state of mind, enabling you to merge your own thinking with that of the philosopher to arrive at a stage when you can build your own beliefs and convictions of life and the dynamics around it.

Don't simply ....
Imagine your Legacy ...
VISUALIZE IT
CREATE IT
PROTECT IT
LOVE IT and ... "LIVE IT".

Some of the Greatest Inventors that transformed this planet to what it is today with all it's splendor and values seemed irrational, ridiculous in their visions and efforts of bringing real value to life through their most innovative creations ... They were cast out by society simply for the reason that the world was way behind them in Consciousness and Intelligence and perceived them as a bunch of people who attempted to build castles in the air.

Yes ... We will look like a crazy group of dreamers to the rest of the world ... As we are in this transit lounge awaiting a migration to this great majestic place that only a few extraordinary people will dare take flight.

"RIGIDLY UNCONVENTIONAL"
LETS go beyond conventional thinking ... lets change ways of acquiring knowledge if its convincing and meaningful to us ... lets work as we read ...
Behind every thought that emerges from within you is an "intention.
LETS PRIMARILY EXAMINE OUR EXISTING INTENTIONS.
Try this one ....
Just silence your conscious mind. ...
What do we really mean by silencing your conscious mind ... you are preparing yourself for absolute naked attention in examining your Intentions ...... devoid from any kind of influence from any of your other mental faculties.

Your mind is detached from your five sensory system ... detached from your unconscious mind and any type of pre-occupations. With these detachments you are connected and functioning with your higher intelligencies. At this stage of consciousness you are examining your intentions in all its purity and truthfulness.

You are not engaged in any kind of thought ... but you will listen with your heart. ... just listen to that subtle voice that talks to you from within.

You wouldn't find this easy because you are trying to silence the most active thinking machine in this whole creation of which you have no control. However it is possible with consistency ..in any environment to silence your mind ...... spend sometime keep trying and trying. Once you have found that emptiness..look for your innermost existing intentions.

So lets examine your intentions. Begin Now ... take a minute or two ....

listen to your ownself. This is an important exercise. You need to accomplish this one ... If you failed, you need to go back. Take a little time more..try again.

Your findings can be among the following;

- You may have discovered that you already do have a crystallized intention with regards to Life's destinations.
- You found out that you really have no clear intention with regards to your life's destination … there are a few indistinct one's.
- Yes it is there in you … fogged..mystified..or even carelessly neglected..not sure … on again off again.

This exercise will reveal to you if you have any contradicting intentions to the new intentions that you are trying to ground. If you do, then you need to go through a weeding process. The reverse process comes in. Now that you are aware of your intentions that will stand as an obstacle or obstruct your thought processes in relation to your new intention, you need to eliminate them.

Eliminating an existing intention should be done with a liberalized mind, in the sense that you free your mind from all intrinsic preoccupations and also all external input that comes from the environment. This is not a meditative process. Your Autonomous will that comes from the executive chamber of your mind empowers you to do this. Just as you do be solemn and totally purified and prepared for adoring whom you believe is the Almighty God, so is this little ritual.

Along with the elimination of your contradictory intentions you need to proclaim your new intention.

JUST answer this question to yourself. What are your new intentions in life.?

Remember an intention is not goal setting … an intention is deep and lies engraved in your unconscious mind …… it can be broad based and can have many goals in- between. Goals are like separate building blocks of a great sky riser.

Here's an example of an intention ….

"I intend moving my life and my work to a new dimension empowering me to serve the planet and its people for many more centuries to come".

Here's an example of a goal statement …

"I would want my company to be listed in the 100 BEST COMPANIES in my country by the end of the next year.

Get into the same state of mind that you were at the eliminating process. Here you are communicating with your innerself, its your power-house, your higher intelligence. It can only hear you if you speak with solemnity, gravity and most of all with utmost belief and trust.

> Having GROUNDED THIS GREAT INTENTION … just as a farmer does nurture his field after the sewing the seed … so should we nurture our INTENTIONS, protecting it from any type of invasion until such time it transforms to be a self defensive device engraved deep within your unconscious mind.

CONTINUOS CONTEMPLATION AND COMPULSIVE MENTAL ACTIVITIES NURTURES AND STRENGTHENS YOUR INTENTIONS PROTECTING IT FROM NEGATIVE INFLUENCES.

.Why examine intentions … why not simply drive toward set goals..?

OUR Minds are vulnerable to invasion..they sway this way and then another way … your goals keep changing as you move along adapting to changing Physiological and Psychological DESIRES …. this is perfectly ok … but remember your intentions which lie deep within you does not easily change along with your conscious mind … so you may end up with a situation where you are consciously moving in a new direction … but deep inside of you, your intentions are in conflict with your movements …… this way you are a split personality …… like two headstrong horses pulling in two different directions … the charioteer is out of control. So it is absolutely important that you examine your intentions and align them in line with your conscious efforts and energies to reach your goals.

Take this important point .... YOUR INTENTIONS GET SUBMERGED BENEATH YOUR UNCONSCIOUS MIND ... once you have made an autonomous choice ...... and exercised your will you have in fact given over the responsibility of its execution to your un-conscious mind.

So set your FOUNDATION RIGHT ....

Set your intentions..backed by your beliefs,Your perceptions meanings and purpose in life.

Represent your intentions and ..stand for it.

REMEMBER ... we here this all the time ... everywhere WHAT YOU INTEND YOU BECOME ....

Truly yes ... but there's a deeper sense behind this Quote ...... Why do we say this ...

A strong intention is supported by your beliefs and your convictions ..they get consolidated with your perceptions your meanings and purposes in life ... and like a prayer automated affirmations and auto-suggestions takes place in your unconscious mind and your conscious mind many times a day..some of them you are aware ... some of them are inadvertent ... we know that our whole metabolism is re-programmable by language word and thought ... and this is what exactly happens when we say ... what you intend you become ... you are really writing your own life's program.

IF THIS PROGRAM IS WRITTEN WITH YOUR AUTONOMOUS CHOICE AND WILL AND WITH INTRINSIC INTENTIONALITY .... YOU HAVE LAID A FOUNDATION THAT CAN SHIFT YOUR LIFE TO A NEW DIMENSION IN TERMS OF CONSCIOUSNESS,INTELLIGENCE AND ABILITIES.

"SO LETS AUTHOR YOUR INTENTIONS

Form a life's credo out of your new intentions ...

Here's an example of a life's credo ...

A CREDO OF an individual with a higher level of Consciousness,Intelligence and Abilities

- *I believe that Legendary Accomplishments are beyond the boundaries of Power, Wealth or Fame.*

- *I believe that I should primarily attire myself with an Adequate Cognitive Instrument to sense, see and realize been a Legacy.*
- *I believe that I could move my life to a new dimension which will empower me to reach astounding heights in life holding my accomplishments with an undying recognition beyond mortal boundaries.*

Use this just as a guide ......

Do it your way, believe me you'll be amazed at your own undiscovered intellect, the depth of your cognitive abilities ... the extents that you can travel in exploring your mental domains to its fullest potentials and how much more that you can do for the planet and its people ...... making it a better place to live in fulfillment.

A great mental foundation is the most important and strategic part of your life. If you build that right ... every other structure will be automatically supported by it.

Many times we attempt to engineer our life, even before we lay our foundation ... and that perhaps is one reason as to why everyone fails to reach GREATNESS .... So lets build our Foundation right, Lets create our Life,s credo which should reflect our intentions.

Many "Visionary thinkers,Thought leaders, Philosophers, philanthropist that walked this planet, continues to remain in our hearts ... We Look up at these great people who have probably sacrificed their material desires and wants, to painstakingly bring true values and meaning to the whole human race.

"As you evolve from one stage to another in your levels of Intelligencies and abilities and elevate from one stage to another in your Social, financial and Professional standards ...... alongside these changes your aspirations in life too takes a change.

That insatiable desire for extraordinary achievements and the hidden unconscious desires to go on and on gets stronger and stronger to the extends of wanting to leave back ......

"Your name echoing across the planet for many centuries to come."

THE MEDIATOR

You make a choice which builds up your intentions and your personality uses your intentions to transform it to reality. Your personality gets characterized by the influence of your beliefs. Intentions that you have stored deep in your unconscious mind shaped and fashioned you to what you are today.

If you keep making irresponsible choices all the time and with many of your intentions colliding with conflicting and contra views, this could be very detrimental, even to the extent of turning you to a kind of a splintered personality, unable to be on course toward a set destination in life ...... In your pursuits of moving your life to a new dimension you need to take into account the consequences of each of your choices. In this sense it is of supreme importance that you make a responsible choice asking yourself several questions for each choice that you make ...

Am I really ready to move? Do I really mean and believe to be a Philanthropist and a legend.?

The mediator between your intentions and the reality, is your personality. Your personality will eliminate the gap between your intentions and its reality. The dynamic of intentions to reality, exist within the world of your existing state of mind.

Are you not metaphorically within your own comfort zone or we may say that garden of Eden. To breakaway from your existing reality ..to create that new Legendary reality ... we need to get our personalities on the job.

For our personalities to be working in line with our intentions directions should come from the executive chamber of our minds ...

if we depend on our ordinary conscious minds, it can work in contradiction to our intentions ... as we have touched on earlier ... minds are vulnerable to many types of invasions. In view of this, delegating this job to our conscious minds can create a war within us.

So it is of paramount importance that we command our personalities from our deepest self ... and that's "YOU" that executive Authority of your life.

"BY NATURE WE ARE A HGHLY SELF CENTERED SPECIES ... THE MORE WE SUCCEED THE STRONGER IS THAT VORACIOUS DESIRE TO HOLD-ON TO OUR POSSESSIONS WILDLY .... THIS GREED OBSTRUCTS US FROM OUR INTENTIONS OF GUIDING THE PLANET AND ITS PEOPLE ...

ELMO QUOTES

'Success' ultimate destination is to leave back our names echoing across the planet for many more centuries to come.

Welcome to a community of " a few extraordinary individuals."

Elmo Quotes

PROTECT YOUR CREATION

ONCE you have flaged your destiny through the power of your Will and intentions which should emerge from the executive chamber of your mind ... you need to protect it from damage, from invasion.

Your creations could be damaged not much from the outside but more from within ... from your own world. So it is of utmost importance that you comprehend your world in its total fullness. To protect your creation of accomplishing legendary heights in life ... primarily you should know your own inner world.

We humans are the most complex and paradoxical creation in the planet. Our total physical realities comprise of bodily functions ... our brains and minds goes to form our mentalities, and deep within us lies our un-conscious minds ... that stores our beliefs, some of which has an unconscious influence in our life's.

Damage to our creations could be caused from any of these faculties. Although your creation of greatness to move your life beyond existing physical and mental limitations has been devoid or liberalized from unconscious intentions ..each time you are struck by a feeling of disbelief relevant to the Legacy you are trying to create ... you'll find your level of confidence deteriorates ...... by nature your mind will begin to support this feeling of failure. So each time you see this reality fading away from your vision..its time you stop to re-build it to its original state..to re-examine your intentions ... to dis-empower your negatives. Just like you rush to a physician when you are in a state of physical discomfort ..you need to freeze all your conscious acts ... acting as your own physician consultant involved in diagnosing very precisely the problem in your mental states ...

re-constructing yourself. There maybe past anxieties, fears, that still remain in your unconscious mind influencing your new conscious efforts of leaving back a Legacy. It is possible that new fears new anxieties can enter. Been conscious about these vulnerabilities and consciously battling them is the key to protect your creation. Re-constructing yourself time and again is of supreme interest in this magnificent journey ... Damage could also be caused by new influences coming from various sources.

You are a pioneer, a creator,an explorer..generally you'll find yourself very lonely battling away your inner conflicts, fears, defending yourself against arrogance ... even against paranoia.

It is beyond doubt that you will encounter new negative influencer's attempting to show you the insensibilty of your dreams.

From the inside your own thought forces attempts to blow you off crowding your vibrance with doubts and de-energizing you most times ...... from the outside you hear demoralizing statements cast at you from your social circle ... perhaps even by your loved ones.You see people gaping at you in astonishment of your preposterous aspirations and efforts. You sense negative vibes all around you ......

"Holding on to the wheel house just like a true bold and daring navigator is the key to legendary accomplishments."

So you need to stand guard by your mind ... screening and filtering all data input reaching you through your sensory system. Data that enters your system should be perceived with a higher level of significance and analyzed with a higher level of understanding.

"The most sophisticated Observatory is located in the Executive chamber of your mind. Its equipped with a remarkably powerful device that enables you to observe your every little mental activity that originates from all your mental faculties ... it has the Authority to think about your mind's own thinking ... check and change thought progressions whenever required. Its your mind's controlling device that can change, switch off or on your mind at its own discretion."

In our terms, its like "The Virtual Chairman of the Board"

Once you have made an Autonomous choice..these negative influences has no power to supersede your creations..the only time that they could successfully do it, is when you permit them to enter your system in negligence and irresponsibility ... Its like a farmer who had toiled laboriously to prepare the ground and sew the seed but not watching over in care.. leaving the weeds to take ground around the plant to destroy its originality. As we know, weeds are unable to stop growth of the plants but they can certainly damage the plant to the extent that it will not produce the expected harvest.. so will it be with our creations.

We may consciously put in so much of energy and effort .... that could be diluted with the negatives bringing down our accomplishments below expected levels.

"Like a stream that shapes and negotiates the fall from the hills and rush down the valleys to be united with the ocean ... so should we adapt ourselves to any given situation maintaining the stability and the power of our minds to navigate us to our destinations."

Elmo Ebert

Exercise Your Liberty

As we know the cerebrum or cortex is the Executive branch of our brains, responsible for making decisions and judgments on all the information coming into it from the body and the outside world. As we are aware, to do its job it performs three distinct functions.

(1) It receives information from the outside world.

(2) Analyzes and compares it with stored information of prior experience and knowledge, and makes a decision;

(3) It then sends its own messages and instructions out to the appropriate muscles and glands.

Our sensory system connects the physical and the psychological worlds and translates them into our experiences.

The primary job of our sensory system is to discard irrelevant stimuli and to select for transmission only that which is relevant. In this situation the first major selection is the biological nature of the senses themselves.

But we do have hundreds of various types of imaginations, thoughts that crosses our minds on a daily basis that emerges from within … which needs to be discarded if not relevant to our intentions in life …… And this process is not an automated process of eliminating irrelevant information as we receive information through our physical senses from the outside world.

THIS NEEDS TO BE DONE THROUGH OUR AUTONOMOUS WILL AND CHOICE.

These rather chaotic, disorganized creations enter and exit haphazardly. Some of them remain for a short while, some are instantly eliminated from your system. These mental drawings are not aligned to your intentions and so they don't get constitutionalized within you, nor are they contributory factors that can guide or advance you toward your intentions of aspiring and realizing legendary heights in life.

Some of these drawings and thoughts are also randomly triggered by spontaneous responses to certain data captured through your senses from the outside world. As an example you may watch a movie and be instantly inspired toward characterizing the hero in the movie ... these spontaneous response are unavoidable ... but they can occupy your mind in destructive thoughts and imaginations ... that could instead be directed toward yourself engaged in mental activities aligned with your intentions.

Although you may attempt to stand guard by your mind ... it is inevitable that many of these negative mental activities can enter your system.

"Despite the fact that it is beyond your power to completely stop negative data entering your mind ...

You are certainly at liberty to exercise your choice and will of halting these inputs from progressing further."

With your intentions so strong and stable toward driving you to move your life and work to a new dimension .... you are powered to stop these un-intended data that enters your mind from further progession. You can eliminate them without reasoning or arriving at any type of decisions through your Executive mind. They will only arouse curiosities and fascinations that will only remain as an external feeling ...... to that extend, they are welcome ...

Pushing boundaries to discover new horizons in life is an heroes errand. Only a few extra-ordinary people are privileged ... and our quest should be to transform ourselves into Masters or Executive Controllers of our life's ...... in this sense entertaining any kind of data is not harmful or destructive toward our road to greatness .... as long as we don't process them any further ...... but exercise our executive choice to only process that which is relevant to move our life to a new dimension in consciousness,Intelligence and Abilties.

Functioning as an extraordinary Individual is been ....

- *Dimensionally,Conscious of our own levels of Consciousness ....*
- *Judgmentally,observing our own behavior ...*
- *Analytically, thinking about our own thinking.*

Engaging in compulsive mental activities of this nature elevates an individual to a mental stature to perceive the world with a higher level of logics and understanding.

WARNING

*Despite the fact that you attempt to stop negative thoughts entering your mind ... just like any progression, during the first stages of your transformation these negative thoughts will penetrate into you ....
At these intital stages it will be beyond your control to stop them ... nevertheless, you are certainly empowered to stop them progressing to detrimental levels.*

This level of consciousness,awareness is what is required to observe and take action appropriately.

Once a negative thought is permitted to progress within you it can take you to disastrous levels like commanding you take a complete turn around from the intended directions that you are progressing with ... perhaps even to the extends of getting you into some kind of aggressive, malicious, revengeful action.

Many of life's blunders originate here. Many of life's great opportunites and breakthrough ideas are missed-out here to be regretted later ... like the old saying goes.."Look before you Leap" in its real sense, its all about observing your thoughts from a higher level of logics and understanding ... and the only way that you can do this ... is in connection with your higher Intelligencies.

A negative thought can enter your mind ... such as disbelief in any non-physical realities that can influence or empower us with new human possibilities ...... now this thought is not in line with our new intentions in life, if you let it progress within ... it will certainly destroy your beliefs and confidence that you have built. With good observation you can stop this negative progression and sustain your positive state of Mind.

To control processing of data we need to view life from a point which lies beyond our physical minds ... in other words we have to stop depending on our rational minds to direct our life. Minds fracture when confronted with certain bodily desires and their psychological counterparts ... they can turn outrageously illogical and irrational in many situations.

At this higher level of consciousness, your personality is powered to detach itself from these Illusions and see it from an higher intelligent perspective. You can live with them ..but still be unaffected by their influences..in simple terms ..no more childish.

These illusions can dis-empower you only when you perceive the world as an ordinary individual ... you are in fact like a de-programmed mind..open to any kind of decision making. Illusions has no power over your higher intelligence that has created its path to greatness with an Autonomous choice and will.

The world is at your disposal. Many great people have put in a lot of energy and effort, with their genius,creating richer and richer environments which we live in today. We should live with them, making us feel good happy and comfortable. Sophisticated technological communication systems could assist us in our endeavors to reach where we want to be ...... but the controlling switch should be within our reach ... in the sense that we can stop them from pushing us to a state of Obsession or addiction that could stand obstructively in our path towards moving our life to a new dimension ... diluting or contaminating our pure intentions.

"Like the wave which is a constituent part of the mighty ocean ...... so are we interwoven into this great fabric of nature and life ... which has no limitations in potentialities and human possibilities."

ELMO EBERT

PART 111

Guiding The Planet
And Its People..

'To guide you need to be at a higher level of consciousness of life and the dynamics around it."

THE MIGRATION

As you transcend into this new dimension in life ... a total transformation takes place in you from the inside to the outside ......

- *From the outside your surface traits and personality transforms to present yourself in society, not as a person of Power, Wealth or fame but of apparent refinement in social etiquette and graceful disposition ......*
- *The world looks up to you in respect and honor ... more than of obligation, fear or subjugation ...*
- *You sparkle out among the crowd and create a positive vibrant environment portraying yourself like a true friend and comforter to everyone who connects to you ...*
- *You are accepted and admired, not as a Business or Political Leader who has the Power to help with expectations of a benefit in return ... but more as a philanthropist who is generously Willing to help.*
- *Inside of you forms a mental and psychological tranquility that maintains within you a balanced temperament at all times*
- *You are empowered to progress with your majestic intentions of serving the planet and its people as a self- actualized individual ...... that will leave back a legacy of your accomplishments for many more centuries to come.*

You and I are privileged to be among ...
"A few Extraordinary Individuals."
Envisioning and contemplating moving an individuals life and work to a new dimension exist beyond the boundaries of an ordinary

mind's visions. By nature,one of our rigid stands is to be where we are, physically and mentally ...... we look for comfort, irrespective of the fact whether they contribute or not toward our personal growth and development.

"COMFORT ZONES ARE OBSESSIVE HIDEOUTS ... ARE FORTIFICATIONS AGAINST CHALLENGES AND OPPORTUNITIES THAT NEEDS AN EXTRA-MILE RUN ... THEY ARE LIKE SKEPTIC ARMORY.'

If you don't take courage to shift your thinking ... you really shut yourself from discovering your true potentialities..tragically you are virtually refusing to engage your total aptitudes to navigate into a new dimension in life.

This courage to leave the present shore to break away from your comfort zone can come to you if you have created that adequate cognitive instrument to magnify your visions and help you to perceive the world with a higher level of significance. Comfort zones, mental infrastructures are created through your beliefs, convictions habits, obsessions and addictions. In order to free yourself ... you need to re-construct yourself ... which means changing your beliefs,habits etc.

"IN ORDER TO MIGRATE, PRIMARILY, YOU NEED TO SENSE, SEE AND FEEL YOUR NEW ENVIRONMENT. VISUALIZE THE ECSTASY OF BEEN THERE ...... WHERE ONLY A FEW DARING,BOLD PEOPLE RESIDE."

Your environments can cage you limiting your aspirations in life. If you are doing alright in your present environment in terms of Social acceptance Financial stability and a great living style within the society that you live, you are likely to cage yourself in this comfort zone. In this compartmentalized state of mind you are leaving out the rest of your potentials unutilized. It is those who really seek who will find. If you don't elevate yourself above your environment in terms of consciousness and higher states of logics and understanding you'll never be able to see new possibilities ... acquire new intelligences and abilities.

In this state of mind you,ll aspire in compatibility to your environmental standards and thinkings ...... the more you are accepted and admired within this environment the more will you cage yourself in comfort and contentment of your accomplishments and attitude toward life and the people around you. A kind of obsession ....

like there's nothing more to think of over and above whats been done ... you work to get better and better in what you do, in simple terms you get richer and richer ...... have more and more control over your immediate environments ... crave for more and more fame, recognition and self-esteem.. ... perhaps you've been influenced by the world around you ... or never took the time or effort to think beyond the frontiers of Power, Wealth and Fame.

As you enter this majestic world of human possibilities which is across the horizon you are like in the darkness ...... but the best part of it is that you are compelled to look for the light ... it is this compulsion which ensures, that you acquire and progress with new intelligencies and new abilities to find your way and excel in this extraordinary environment which seems irrational, impractical even like non-sensical.

"One of the most bold and daring challenges that we can face and conquer is to shift into an unknown arena with belief and conviction ...... and find ways of excelling within this arena reaching legendary heights, no matter what adversities comes our way".

The quest to sustain your accomplishments with an undying recogntiton requires you to be holding yourself with an extraordinary level of Self-Esteem, perceiving life beyond it's mortal limitations.

IN ORDER TO CREATE AND BRING ALIVE AN INNOVATIVE IDEA THAT CAN RESULT IN A POSITIVE TRANSFORMATION TO THE WHOLE HUMAN RACE ... MOVING TO A NEW DIMENSION IN TERMS OF CONSCIOUSNESS AND INTELLIGENCE ... BECOMES A CATEGORICAL IMPERATIVE.

Elmo " *The Conscious Evolutionnaire*"

WHEN THE DEEPEST OF YOU IS ENGAGED

When it comes to paintings..we can never miss out the name of Leonardo da vinci …… Mona Lisa and the last supper particularly mesmerized the world. But 'there is something more about this great painter. He was a "Renaissance Man." He had an amazing insight for science, who has a military engineer, visualized devices beyond the scope of his time.

How is it that he astonished the world with his paintings.?

It's not one's competencies and skills relevant to a certain task that make's one great … it is the engagement of your deepest self that brings in the appropriate competencies and skills to execute a task at an extra-ordinary level.

Despite the fact that most people are engaged in various professions, working untiringly, it doesn't mean that one can reach out to accomplish extra-ordinary results in a given task.

When the deepest part of you is engaged … this existing intelligence that one has, breaks boundaries to discover new intelligencies and new abilities.

This is a stage, a level of Meta- Motivation … when you are doing things as a self actualized individual..your drives here are your passions … your determination to do it is beyond mental energy … your heart is involved … all your mental faculties are integrated just as a team of specialist developing an extra-ordinary device that can save the whole of mankind.

You connect yourself into your deepest part when your intentions, your thought forces and your heart are moving and working in one direction. This inter-connection is that mystical energy that powers you beyond the level of your competencies and skills to reach legendary heights in whatever you do.

Scientific experts are producing remarkable consistent findings across a wide array of fields. *It is now understood that talent doesn't mean intelligence, motivation or personality traits .... Its an innate ability to do some activity instinctively and intrinsically.*

This process of connecting to your deepest self should begin with you disempowering your other influences that are not in line with your intentions of been a legend. You have got to attune your mind to the required frequency. Imagine your mind as a powerful receiving station with your brain as the receiving device ...... we have got the greatest gift of all..our Autonomy of choice and liberty to attune our minds to any channel. So firstly its your conscious effort to keep your mind attuned to this greatness channel. As you know just as atmospheric disturbances causes distortion in transmitting data ..so does our own mental transmitters..they will sway here and there causing a significant distortion in your attempt to be attuned with clarity. This awareness is the primary key to be connected to your deepest self. Now that your intentions are clear ... a conscious effort should be made to keep yourself attuned in thought and imaginations and action. It is as if you have all the time got your fingers on the remote controller of your mental receiving station.

With this deliberate compulsive attention of keeping yourself attuned all the time, ... it gradually turns out to be transformed to an automatic mental activity and you arrive at a point of time ... when you can be attuned without a conscious effort. Compulsive mental activities transforms into automated mental activities just as habits do turn into neurological pathways. Once this attunement is automated, your thought forces are connected to your deepest self, where ...... *your intentions are firmly engraved.*

The heart is our most valuable life organ, that also functions as a center of intelligence other than our brains. Researches claim that the heart plays a role in the functioning of human intelligence, emotions and personality. Beside been a blood pumping vessel that keeps us a live, the heart is an emotional organ that has a relationship with the brain and our deepest self. Your deepest self is a form of infinite energy. Its not like a thinking machine such as a mind as we know..it is an entity of a higher order of logics and understanding and will relate and connect only to an entity or energy form of its same constitution.

We are five sensory personalities and our logics and understandings originate in our minds. If we are to elevate ourselves to this higher level connecting ourselves to our deepest part becomes a definite move.

It is only our heart that is capable of perceiving the world through a higher level of significance,a higher level of logics … which means that in whatever we do in pursuit of moving to a new dimension in life, we need to involve our feelings emotions … which is our heart.

When we are seeking simple ways or practical ways of accomplishing legendary heights, it seems totally irrelevant to be engaging our hearts. This is the distinction..this is what makes the difference between the ordinary and the extra-ordinary individual.

We can energize our thoughts and actions with our feelings.. our emotions. This way your mind works in collaboration with your heart, your thoughts are energized, screened, filtered and purified to the extent that this integrated power connects you to the deepest part of you … where everythings possible … where the required intelligence knowledge and skills to reach these hights are showered on you.

INTO THE UNKNOWN

    Adventuring into the unknowns of life does not help us with past or present knowledge and guidelines ...... we hover in the darkness with only our intuitional and instinctual powers and our advanced mental powers such as intuition and precogniton that prompts to protect and help us sense and capture what seems to be an impossibility to an individual of an ordinary mind, disposition and attitude.

    Only a few are privileged to board this vessel ... and the criteria for reservations is not based on wealth power or fame ... but on belief and that burning desire to move one's life to a new dimension..

Wealth power and fame are great external achievements and possessions that brings an individual
recognition and glory ......

But it is accomplishment beyond these boundaries
that distinguishes and recognizes an individual as a
legend ...... for many centuries to come.

ELMO EBERT

A GREAT NEW HABIT

Just as you have now created an adequate mental instrument to move you to a new dimension in life and your profession, it is inevitable that you'll develop a new mental habit related to your intentions.

There are physical habits and then again there are mental habits. Your physical habits can be ... set times for your meals, a time for exercising, reading etc. Your existing mental habits can be that you habitually keep thinking of past experiences or future dreams that you wish to realize in life ...... just as affirmations and auto-suggestions ...... compulsive mental engagements relevant to your primary intentions help in realizing the ultimate objectives of your primary or other intentions.

Metal habits and thoughts are two different engagements. Thoughts emerge randomly depending on the situation ... example you see, read or hear of something that reminds you of your intentions of moving your work to a new dimension. Here you are engaged in these relevant thoughts and you progress with them. In the case of a mental habit you make it a point deliberately to be engaged in these thoughts at a most suitable time of the day, which in your experience is the best time for breakthrough ideas to come your way.

During this time slot you contemplate on your legendary aspirations and destinations and further with the integration of all your mental faculties Conscious/unconscious and subconscious minds. You visualize that new cognitive instrument and virtually create them with the power of your Autonomous will and choice. This is a kind of mental exercise ... with many repetitions ...... day after day ... time after time these thoughts transforms you empowering you with this new cognitive instrument. Gradually, although you may not realize it in the initial stages, you find yourself struck with some unimaginable thoughts coming your way ... of possibilities that seemed really impossible to you before you began this new mental habit.

This is not about simply thinking ...
- *Its about capturing promptings and guidance from your higher intelligence ...*
- *Its analyzing these thoughts with a higher level of significance ...*
- *Its arriving at new beliefs and convictions showered down to you from a source beyond your rational mind or by your pragmatic thinking skills.*

Just paint a picture of your NEW COGNITIVE INSTRUMENT ...... use not your rational mind ... but the power of your Mental Creations Vivid Imaginations and Visualizations.

Find the most conducive environment find the most constructive favorable time and build this great habit..the results you,ll find to be amazing.

Just like any other habit that you newly began ... you'll find this habit on and off for a while ... then it begins to get better and better disciplined. Consistency and solemnity in this habit is a categorical imperative for best results.

Yes, ... this will seem like "castles in the air" to an ordinary mind, but only a few are privileged to be in this state of belief and this state of consciousness ... this is very precisely what distinguishes the ordinary from the extraordinary.

The adequate Cognitive instrument that we create is an advanced non-physical mental faculty. What is mental ... what is non-physical can only be created through a nonphysical device ... this way there is compatible communication ... you cannot communicate with a non-physical reality with a physical entity ... for example your physical brain cannot give rise to an extraordinary cognitive instrument on its own. As we touched on earlier our brains ... our physical mind and our non-physical mind constitutes our total mental domain. Its the emanation of electro-magnetic energy from our brains that creates our mind and extends to our non-physical mind. The mind which is created by our brains is an automated process ... in other words you have no control in this development process, it's a natural growth passage. The activation of the non-physical mind is not an automated process and needs to be nurtured and requires compulsive mental activities to be connected to this non-physical faculty ...... so you cannot depend on your brain to create this non-physical Mind that will take you to a higher level of logics and understandings.

The process, as an example is like the wax the flame and light of a lit –up candle. The flame which is like the mind ... resurrects from the wax which is like the brain ... and the light which is like the non-physical mind resurrects from the Flame ...... so we see these constituent parts symbiotic and synergistic to give out the best in its ultimate measure.

In fact may I boldly say that our brain is a biological human organ and only enables one to capture identify all influx through our five sensory system ...... and let's the mind progress with analysis and findings.

For many decades there has been several definitions and arguments about the distinction between the brain and the mind ... however it is an accepted fact that the brain is a physical component and the mind a non-physical. Despite the fact that Stimulation of the brain organ can bring about situational, temporary bodily and mental changes ...... but brain stimulation cannot cause permanent changes in your source traits or surface traits disposition or attitudes ... it is only physical damage to the brain that can cause these changes.

However through compulsive mental activities it is possible to change everything in you.

"Today, Nobody is the ultimate Authority or expert in the science of Life. Perhaps as the whole human race evolves in the distant future, we may sense, see comprehend and define the true meaning of life and the dynamics around with higher intelligence. We need to go by with whatever intelligence we possess as at today."

"WE CHOOSE TO BE GREAT ... BECAUSE IT IS DARK AND WINDING TO THE TOP."

Legendary acomplishments in life are beyond that which springs out of Power Wealth or fame ...... it originates from a higher source of intelligence, wisdom or deep emotional feelings of care or sympathy toward the whole human race, that triggers inventions or innovative thoughts and philosophies that can bring sollace and happiness to the depressed and the suffering.

An individual, necessarily need not be in a state of high financial or socially powerful standing to be engaged in activities of a legendary nature ...... you can do this in the most sophisticated majestic mansion in the city or in a countryside cottage ...... Either way it gives you immense pleasure to be serving the world and its people bringing them human values and contentment in varying degrees irrespective of the fact of who or where they come from ...... this moves your greatness beyond mortal limitations ...

"leaving back your good name echoing gloriously across the planet for many centuries to come."

BUILD YOUR OWN BELIEFS.

I am addressing my views to a few extra-ordinary individuals and my approach is a self directive exercise and not a conventional step by step progressive methodology.

This gradual progress should find you moving upward driven by your own convictions, from that initial stages of curiosities and fascinations to comprehend and believe leading you to actual practice in seeking connections to your sub- mental faculties ... empowering you with new intelligencies and abilities.

A philosophy of any nature can only leave you with a deep thought provoking state of mind, enabling you to merge your own thinking to arrive at a stage when you can build your own beliefs and convictions.

KEEP YOUR CELESTIAL SWITCH–ON

Imagine your mind as a receiving device such as one in an astronomical center ...... attuned and engineered to capture any attempts of communication from the Universe and programmed to read the language of the Universe.

Despite the fact that you may listen to some sounds through this device ...... If you don't understand the language of communication ... the device is of no use.

Presumably the Universe has its language that it depicts through various systems of formations in the skies that still remains incomprehensible to our dull and primitive faculties ... Perhaps in the future ... yes we will evolve to the extent that everything that's in the skies do have a meaning that can be interpreted.

Its only if you switch-on your non-physical or higher mental faculty to receive ... that you will hear a subtle voice as if from above that attempts to prompt you with an intelligence that you cannot understand with your logical/rational mind. It is the encompassing of these non-physical faculties that empowers you to move ahead of the rest.

These promptings comes to you also inadvertently and they leave you without much progress. You need to be extremely observant of these communications, acknowledge them and progress with them.

This is what transforms you to a multi-sensory personality from a five sensory system ... this is what will differentiate you ... empowering you to move your work and life to a new dimension.

Many times in life you,ll find yourself ... really extraordinary, as if you been energized with a new realization, new insight new intelligencies surrounds you. Suddenly you feel so great ... a feeling of intellectual invincibility.

Contemplate this ... analyze as to how you got there ... into this higher state of logics and understandings ... into this higher state of physical and mental healthiness..this feeling of confidence courage and excellent skills and competencies. Most times you will discover for yourself, that this comes to you when your conscious mind is liberalized from its environment, and although inadvertantly ..you are also liberalized from the influences of your unconscious mind. The feeling here is one of lightness, contentment, feeling fulfilled. this is a point when you need to be at your best capturing data that rush into your mind. This is the extraordinary and the controlling switch to move your life to a new dimension that can empower you to perform at astounding heights.

THE CONSCIOUS EFFORT

The mind is a thinking thing, so thought is the real essence of the mind. The mind can be thought to be like a complex piece of software implemented in the hardware of the brain.

Although a thought seem a non-physical energy ...... thoughts are forms generated by energy that are shaped by consciousness. So if there is no consciousness there is no thought ... just like certain lower levels in life forms.

We use our consciousness to generate thoughts. Now that we have used our autonomous will to move our life and our profession to a dimension that empowers us to capture data from a wider dynamical zone than that of our existing five sensory footprint ... we must let our thought forces be focused on this creation. Conscious thoughts can be triggered in many ways. You can use your senses to trigger thoughts for example ... if you have your Life credo displayed in your office room ... each time you take a glimpse in the midst of your daily activities ... it will help you to generate thought forces that's relevant to your life's ultimate intentions.

You can use your auditory faculty as well..example .... you have created a sound ..a particular sound of nature..let us say..birds flying, winds blowing, rivers flowing.. ... which you have created a psychological link to your new world ... Each time your attention is focused in consciously listening to these sounds it will generate thought forces in relation to your intentions of introducing to the world a philosophy that will help and support the whole human race to live a life of contentment and fulfillment in whatever social or financial standing they exist.

"BUILD UP AN ENVIRONMENT RELEVANT TO YOUR GREAT INTENTIONS.
LET THE ENVIRONMENT PROMPT YOU TO GET INTO DEEP THOUGHT …
FINDING WAYS AND MEANS OF MOVING YOUR LIFE AND YOUR WORK TO A
NEW DIMENSION. YOUR OFFICE, YOUR HOME, YOUR CAR YOUR "GET LOSS
PARADISE" THEY CAN ALL BE TRANSFORMED TO SUPPORT YOU TO REALIZE
YOUR NEW ASPIRATIONS IN LIFE."

EMPOWER YOURSELF AS IF ITS YOUR RESPONSIBILITY TO GUIDE THE
WORLD AND ITS PEOPLE TO A BETTER LIFE.

EMPOWER YOURSELF AS IF YOU ARE DELEGATED THE JOB OF LEAD-
ING THE WORLD TO A NEW DIMENSION IN PERCEPTION, LOGICS AND
UNDERSTANDINGS.

EMPOWER YOURSELF AS IF THE WORLD AND ITS PEOPLE URGES FOR YOUR
WISDOM AND GUIDANCE FOR MANY MORE GENERATIONS TO COME.

The most emotionally touched humanitarian deeds are sacrifi-
cial … they caused physical or mental pain or psychological stress
to the giver momentarily ……

These legendary deeds in all its glory brings solace to the depressed and needy … and is beyond malicious intentions of gaining
Power Wealth or Fame.

Elmo Quotes

RE-DEFINING DISCIPLINE

Legendary accomplishments were realized by a few extraordinary individuals who perspired tirelessly in body and mind to amazing extends.
This amazing discipline in them even changed their total anatomical conception ... in the sense that they were individuals who could have shred their bodily desires and wants such as sleep or food to continue to engage themselves in whatever they were focussed on with the same levels of concentration and enthusiasm.

Yes, we all need to be disciplined to achieve what we want in life ... a wake up call, time for coffee, tea, time for work, for rest for family.

The journey toward legendary accomplishmets requires a discipline of a different nature ... the difference is what matters most ... separating the ordinary from the extra-ordinary. In the pursuit of shifting to a new dimension ... most of our efforts and energies are engaged in deep thought. ... creating ... exploring ...... pioneering a few concepts and breakthrough ideas in whatever we are seeking..

The discipline we require here is not governed by time ... but is summoned by the readiness of your mind or specifically by your total self.

So discipline here does not mean sticking to a certain work schedule..'...

but obeying that command that comes from deep within .... as if an inner voice saying "Are you ready".

This command comes to you when your mind is liberalized ... as if everything is over and its free to work on your most constructive engagement ... exploring possibilities of discovering the bridge that can take the world across to a new dimension in purposeful and meaningful living.

To those who seek greatness in their work ... this obedience to this command is real discipline. At this call you are connected to your deepest self .... and the discipline you require is to put away everything else ... to attend to your work no matter what important engagements are in your hands, you need to free yourself to give heed to this most important call.

As long as you are connected with this higher state of mind ... you need to have the discipline to stay with it .... as long as it takes. In everyday life we call this moment ... Intuitional promptings ... gut feelings ... instincts or in more simpler terms ... something's triggering inside of me.

These summons comes to you very regularly ... unlike to an ordinary mind ... the fact been that you have already created an adequate mental instrument within you with your strong will and choice and deep intentions. Although initially they may come to you at most unexpected times ... like deep into the night these calls will eventually come to you in a most organized manner ... at regular times in the day. The important thing here is to obey and follow instructions ... it is as if the thinking is done by somebody elsewhere and you are simply making a note of it in your mind. You will be amazed at the breakthrough ideas that will come your way to help and support you to reach greatness in whatever you do. You should be disciplined to stay along with this altered state of consciousness.

We human beings have much greater power than we are conscious of ... but we find it extremely difficult to lay aside our personalities to allow us to be attuned to this universal source of knowledge.

Are we disciplined enough to detach ourselves from our personalities to receive these powers.?

This is the differentiation in the discipline that I'm talking about. There is nothing occult or paranormal or psychic about this ... you will not experience it if you don't have a human device adequate enough to receive what is offered.

So lets be disciplined in its real sense. ... to prepare ourselves with the beliefs and awareness all the time, any place, under any circumstances.

We cannot go on pretending day by day imagining that you can perform feats of a legendary nature with a few simple steps to follow ... believing that you can read listen and watch inspirational stories of the greats. We can fill in volumes and volumes of inspiring tales that will hype you up for the moment.. ignite you from within ... set you on. ... like on fire ... but lets be real here ...... can we sustain this state of positivity at a constant non-diminishing mental state.?

LETS NOT LOOK FOR THE MOST PRACTICAL OR SIMPLEST WAYS OF GETTING THERE ... LETS NOT USE A VOCABULARY THAT IS MODERN OR STYLISH OLD OR NEW FASHIONED ... LETS DO IT THE RIGHT WAY AND THE TRUE WAY ... NO MATTER HOW WEIRD YOU MAY SEEM OR SOUND.

There are two ways that we receive information through sounds.

One: They come from the outside..through our hearing sense ... and most of these sounds and hearings are unavoidable..we have no control of hundreds of sounds that enter our minds and most of them are of no value or meaning to us.

The second is our deliberate listening where we intentionally engage ourselves giving ear to the information that is coming in many forms. This is all coming through our auditory system. But the discipline we require here is of a different nature. Here you are not listening to the usual sounds that resonate through sound waves ... but to a subtle voice that is attempting to communicate with you through your mind via your heart.

In this sense we need to generate a two way communication system. Just like we dial a telephone number to speak to one of our loved one's ... here we need to prepare ourselves with this new discipline ... this new habit of liberalizing our minds to listen to this voice.

This great human faculty which we now refer to as intuition, gut feeling etc ... we have lost with lack of belief and engagement. Our

dependency on our five sensory system has left this faculty dormant. Only the extraordinary opens himself to receive this call ... only the extra-ordinary will discipline himself to trust this call ......
This is what differentiates the greats from the rest.

Today you stand out as a Chairman,a Director of a large Corporate, A renowned Professional, A scientist ... or an extraordinary Individual. This does not mean, that you have arrived at the final destination of your success story.

Genuine Success should continue beyond material achievements with an undying recognition. It's ultimate destination is immortality cosmocentricity ......

"Leaving back your name echoing across the planet gloriously for centuries to come."

How The Greats Practice

You maybe a Renowned professional contemplating an Innovative Principle on life and success, or a highly recognized Corporate leader venturing into the most unique product the world has seen ...... Exploring new ways of doing it is what makes the difference.

Perspiration in mind and body, as we know is the strongest drive to succeed ...... This perspiration is the ability to move from failure to failure with the same enthusiasm and inner drive. It is that power to rise from failure that is the key element to greatness ...... We need to practice ceaselessly to attune our minds for originating .... creating ... exploring even when we are physically engaged, keeping our minds on the run.

When you are attired with an adequate cognitive human instrument, you will conceive every bodily movement and every mental activity with a higher level of significance ...... This new dimension in practice is the consistent attunement of your mind to this higher level of logics and understanding ... it's like igniting the torch each time the fire blows away.

Just like one is attempting to attune a radio to a certain frequency under stormy conditions which causes disruption to clarity in reception ...... so is the frequency that we are attempting to capture ... we require to practice our mental habits under very high stormy conditions ... this practice requires us to pay absolute naked attention in what we are doing.

There were many who achieved great heights with this conscious effort. Although initially you may find it difficult to have your mind set in this direction ... with consistent conscious effort this attunement gets constitutionalized into your system.

Moving your practice or your work sessions into a new dimension is getting better and better in what you do .... to finally move you out of the crowd ... functioning at an extraordinary height in intelligences and abilities which empowers you to perform Legendary accomplishments.

Practice reaches a new dimension when body and mind moves in harmonious partnership toward an intended destination. This great inter-dependency reaches a point of peak performance .... a point where you feel that everything's possible. Suddenly the greatest breakthrough ideas hits you from nowhere, you have surpassed your restricted levels of performance and moved to new heights in human possibilities.

Practice takes a positive transformation when the body and mind are equally engaged in the task ... not simply to have a positive mental attitude ... but to attune yourself into an explorative body-mind combination ... This body mind inter-dependency, and harmonious partnership is that spark that is required to move to legendary heights in whatever you do. With this integrated power. You are functioning as the executive authority of your life.

So lets be alive at work and practice .... lets practice to discover new horizons in human potentials.

This is what makes the difference ..this is the attitude and the approach that makes you " spark" out to reach where only a few extraordinary individuals dare.

Let's merge our thinking, perhaps, team-up to lead the world to a new dimension in Human possibilities.

"Life is a drama ... more of Agonies than ecstasies ... the more you are empowered to face and challenge adversities the more are your chances for Success in life. "

Elmo Ebert.

The higher you aspire in life the stronger are the winds of disaster that will blow against you .... this awareness and the readiness in mental stature to face them is the key to accomplishing astounding heights in success .... The more you overcome these challenges the stronger you grow mentally from stage to stage.

Your vivid imaginations and visualizations of your destination becomes more and more crystalized ENERGIZING you with utmost confidence and determination to be there.

It reaches a point of reality that you feel within you ...... which transforms you to an "Invincible Intellect" in this particular journey.

You experience the ecstasy and glory of touching that finishing line even before you reach it.

"ADVERSITIES DON'T HIT YOU ... THEY AWAKEN YOU AND GIVE YOU THE OPPORTUNITY TO REACH LEGENDARY HEIGHTS IN LIFE"

PICKING UP THE PIECES

In the process of this quantum shift in your mind and your activities of transcending to a new dimension ...... it is inevitable that time after time winds of disaster will blow you off your feet regardless the fact that you try to keep yourself grounded. Some of these adverse conditions can dis-empower your will to turn them to opportunities of revealing your genius. Moving your work to a new dimension needs muscle and mind.

When you lay on the ground in mental stature picture yourself as if hit by an opponent in a heavyweight boxing fight ...... picture you lying on the canvass ... you can hear your people scream ... wake up ... wake up ...... in the midst of all this you also hear a subtle voice from within saying ...".This is not real ... you are on the test .... just wake up and fight."

When a burning desire is transformed into a deliberate obsession,a deliberate addiction ... every other happenings around it becomes unreal ... even up to the extent of most disastrous adversities in your life this yearning to move yourself into a new dimension in whatever you do remains in you strong as an invincible intellect.

When you are down..observe the dramatic event from an elevated standpoint ... here you are a dual personality ... you are the actor and the director of the drama ... you are the front stage performer and the backstage mechanism. You are in control of this whole drama and can navigate it to your own direction.

Your minds got the power to create this dual personality.

As the controller of this dramatic event you let your shadow personality or your actor personality go through the emotions the feelings the agony of been down.

"AS LONG AS YOU ARE DETACHED FROM THE DRAMA YOU WILL RETAIN THE POWER TO CONTROL IT ... PICK UP THE PIECES ... RE-CONSTRUCT THE TRUE "YOU" RE-CONSTRUCT THIS POWERFUL CHARACTER .... BUT IF YOU ARE INSTITUTIONALIZED INTO THIS ACTOR- CHARACTER YOU WILL LAY ON THE GROUND UNABLE TO RE-ASSEMBLE YOURSELF."

The important thing here is that you have to engineer this creation at times when your mind is ready for it and not wait to do it in the midst of a storm. Minds functions at its best in times of tranquility and fractures in times of turbulence.

When you create your dual personality at times when your mind is liberalized from any kind of pre- occupation..along with your autonomous will and intentions this creation becomes real and with repeated consultation with your higher personality you automatically elevate yourself above an ordinary state of intellectualism.

This makes the difference ...... creating a dual personality to protect you when you are down.

Creating a dual personality seems to be an unrealistic,impractical effort when we perceive the world with our ordinary mind ...... but with an adequate mental instrument that enables us to perceive the world with a higher level of significance .... this is a reality ... these are true human instruments that remain undiscovered in ignorance or in dis-belief.

Your shadow personality is like a secret hero casting a light in every step you take,ensuring that you are moving in your intended direction. He's like a mentor who will stand by you all the time.

Cultivating this new habit of consulting your secret hero at times of adversity ... is not only a mental process ... but a physical connection as well ... Habits are formed by neuro biological interaction driven by intentions and supported by thought forces. As we intend to develop a new habit and consistently engage in this act we send electro chemical messages along neural pathways. Doing this over and over again strengthens this biological or physical connection, until it turns out to be an automated function in your neurological system. This is the point which a permanent habit is created. Thoughts alone don't give rise to new habits. However everything is first originated in the workshop of the mind before they become a reality.

I wish I had a few easy simple steps to show you how you could take your work to a new dimension..sorry I don't and I don't believe that anyone else could do that for me.

Reaching beyond ordinary levels requires the will to Pioneer ... originate ... create an attitude that's daring with an explorative mind..consolidated with the will to sweat your body and mind.

We are very much a part of all nature ...... just like natural disasters that comes along once a while..it is a natural process that we get hit by a storm that gets us mentally imbalanced ...... it is only the ignorance of this expectation that could break us to pieces ... but as long as you have this foreknowledge ... this foresight ...... this higher level of logics and understanding. you can always" Pick up the Pieces".

"The higher and higher you aspire and reach out on this legendary journey, the more stronger and bitter are the adverse storms that attempts to obstruct your progress .... Only a few extraordinary individuals such as you and I can hold on to our visions, despite these piercing invasions from all around us."

By an endless preoccupation and attachment with the past, we are missing out on the discovery of true human potentails.

Its time that we re-examine our existing beliefs and convictions and shift our perceptions to a higher level of logic and understanding.

ELMO EBERT

THE GREATEST COMMITMENT

With the exception of now and again a great spiritual leader who possessed an extreme compassionate heart walking this planet ...... We humans are in its deepest sense..Self centered very lonely individuals..

Making a serious commitment to your ownself is by far the strongest commitment that an individual can ever get into. Committing yourself to move your life to a new dimension is as serious as offering your life for this reward.

So many stories tells us of great people and of how they went to the extents of sacrificing their material desires in life to fulfill their commitment to themselves. Of most people we know of.. they reached where they wanted to be ... the biggest attribution been that unconditional pledge to themselves.

Making a commitment to move our world to a new dimension in the absence of foreknowledge is as daring and heroic as a journey to the unknowns of life. The passion the determination for Pioneering, creating, exploring are the only attributes that can move you to greatness..what is known, what is clearly seen or achievable is not a heroes playfield.

Compromising, sacrificing your material desires,your psychological desires and your ego driven life styles becomes a must. Like I have said earlier..in the pursuit for a legendary accomplishment, you find yourself singled out lonely ..perhaps even to the extent of been discriminated at times by society and even family. You will not look visible..they perceive you only from the outside ... and then there's nothing great about you that they see ... up to a point when the world is wanting to talk to you ... and would talk about you for centuries ahead when what you have done has given real value to the whole human race in various ways..when you set a benchmark that everyone wants to reach.

UNTIL SUCH TIME YOU ARE REQUIRED TO SWEAT YOUR MIND AND BODY.. TO HOLD BACK THE TEARS IN TIMES OF ADVERSITIES..TO CRUSH YOUR EGOIC INFLUENCE..TO BE UNASHAMED OF DISCRIMINATIONS..TO DROWN SADNESS WHEN YOU ARE LONELY ....THERE IS NO OTHER SIMPLE WAYS TO LEAVE BACK A LEGACY.

The commitment made to yourself comes from the depth of you ... you need to re-identify yourself. Imagine you have been transformed ...... in the sense that you are unable to go back to your past ... you stand as a full human with all its potentialities, you have been given the liberty to move your life in any direction you want it to move ......

Moving into the unknowns have no scientific facts, no signpost, the past don't give any worthy statistics or facts guiding you to the future ...... or to your destination. Everything of the past knowledge, experiences, know-how's is no more of value.

There's just one guide ... that's 'YOU" the deepest part of you. Motivating you every step of the way ... with your BELIEF'S ... driving you with your Autonomous Choice and Will ... empowering you with a new cognitive instrument to navigate the unknowns ... giving foresight to take a glimpse of what lies beyond the horizons.

"Today leaders are making policy decisions based on intuitional promptings, gut-feelings as well as rationality ...... A new age has dawned ... a few extraordinary people will lead the world into this new era."

ELMO ... Conscious Evolutionnaire

ADVERSITIES REVEALS GENIUS

Most greatest accomplishments were performed at moments of adversities. Unexplored, treasured latent powers emerges like from nowhere to crush or eliminate adversities.

The key point here is that it needs a kind of triggering of some sort to connect ourselves to our hidden or undiscovered powers. Adversities brings about fear, shame, threat etc … that triggers this connection. Working pro-actively or with this foreknowledge means, not simply wait for adversities … but find an alternate to let this power flow.

So what options do we have.?

LETS REPLACE FEARS OF LOOSING WITH A BOLD AND DARING ATTITUDE AND THE WILL TO RISK IN ORDER TO EXPLORE THE UNKNOWN

LETS REPLACE SHAME WITH A NON-EGOIC DETERMINED APPROACH TOWARD GREATNESS.

Just as adversities reveals genius … so should we go looking for our genius by engaging ourselves in challenging task with initiation … rather than wait for challenges.

As you get yourself caged in your comfort zone routinally engaged in your activities you are deprived of exploring many other possibilities … your latent powers remains unknown to you. So you live battling life with still an undiscovered power … obviously your battles are tuff …… you are on again..off again … feeling great at one moment and feeling like nothingness in another.

Make a bold move … stop been completely dependent on your existing competencies, skills academic backgrounds your everything what you are as at today … imagine you have lost all that and you are left only with "YOU".There is a challenge ahead of you which cannot be faced with any of your existing competencies skills or intelligence. You need a new kind of intelligence..a new type of ability to face these challenges. Here you have no other option but to enroll yourself into a new academy..this academy where everything is possible..where genetic transference does not matter..where riches does not matter ... where environments does not matter..whether you are from a world power or a third world country, doesn't give any advantage the other ... here's where "YOU" come in ... where you confront challenges to reach greatness..not with your present skills or competencies or intelligence or knowledge..but on your Autonomous choice and will ...... bringing true value and fulfilling living to the whole human race ...... moving your accomplishments beyond its mortal limitations, giving it an undying recognition and leaving back your name gloriously for many more centuries to come.

You just choose what you want to be. You may choose to be a scientist and serve the world within the scientific frame of knowledge and understanding through relevant educational streams .... you may also choose to serve the world through a non-scientific explorative search for the unknown facts of the world ... either way legendary acccomplishments is within your reach in whatever you do. You may use the laws of the land as a qualified lawyer to defend people in court or you can use your inner wisdom to mentor and counsel people toward leading a life of righteousness with morality and high human values, keeping them away from legal issues ...... either way "The world will remember you"

Begin to believe, trust your inner Academy..where everythings' possible ... you can enroll yourself to any program of your choice .... from the outside you got knowledge from the great Universities.. who will take you to the level of a doctorate in any discipline ... from the inside your great mentors and magnificent teachers are domicile in the depths of your being who will incessantly guide you to a state, transforming you to an extraordinary individual with true humanistic values extending your hand to bring worth to every human being in the planet liberalized from any worldly assessments or demographics.

Pursuing legendary accomplishments is not for the conservatives the skeptics not for the weak in the mind..its not the playing ground of the rational logical thinker ... or the scientific fact seeker..its an heroes play ground ... a daring explorers driving seat ... its the favorite arena of the adventurous mind.

In order to move your life to a new dimension you need an adequate cognitive instrument that will empower you to get there.You cannot incorporate this extraordinary instrument into your life if your beliefs and convictions has the slightest doubt on its existence.

These possibilities has to be primarily designed and constructed in your mind helping and supporting you to build an insatiable desire and act upon its construction with indestructible enthusiasm.

Only a few extraordinary people continues their success beyond Material accomplishments leaving back the glory of their success and their names ...

FOR MANY CENTURIES TO COME

We are flamboyant and ecstasized at moments of physical or mental positive states ... they appear and disappear like a screen in a movie ... and at times of depression we lose all that hype and feel like shameful embarrassed looses.

Retaining these moments of ecstasies and state of mind is the key to greatness. To understand this we need to explore the depths of our potentialities in its fullness.

It's a vain effort to be battling these varying mental states from the surface. We are shaped and fashioned by a back stage mechanism that lay deep within us ... although we may attempt to play the role of a great hero on the front stage ... we may look like clowns in the eyes of the audience if our front stage act is not aligned with our back stage mechanism.

Exercise the liberty to be great. Extrapolate, projecting yourself into the future, where you stand as a legend. Experience that feeling as you visualize yourself and confirmly proclaim to yourself ......

"That's where I belong"

Despite the fact that you may, as at today not be having the required intelligence and abilities or you are not in that level of consciousness to realize this creation ... you should be inspired and driven by the fact that your intentions, choice will and your fierce conscious efforts to get there,is beyond doubt, continuously moving you to a higher level of significance in perception and at the same time elevating you to a higher state of consciousness.

Perhaps, initially it may seem to be an unrealistic,impractical realization ... however, as you move deeper and deeper widening your vision, crystallizing your thinking, seeing the world with a higher level of significance, knowing you in your total humaneness ...... then you will experience a whole world of possibilities opening up right before your eyes..this visibility will inspire and drive you to a point of no return ... when you see yourself standing among a few extra-ordinary people, leaving a legacy back.

Remember ... In this whole journey into the unknown ... you are left with just one indomitable power..,and that's your belief ... like the pair of wings of a bird. If you ever drop these wings that's holding you up right along the way .... it's a categorical imperative that you need to re-construct yourself before you proceed with this journey.

The only way that you can hold on to your beliefs and convictions is through a total transformation in your Disposition and your bold and daring attitude to explore the unknowns of life.

THE INVINCIBLE MENTAL ATTIRE

BELIEF ... THE BRIDGE THAT MOVES THE ORDINARY TO THE EXTRA-ORDINARY ......

BELIEF ...... THE FOUNDATION ON WHICH LEGENDS ARE BUILT.

BELIEF ...... THE DRIVING FORCE THAT KEEPS YOU ON COURSE IN THE ABSENCE OF FACTS TO GUIDE YOU

BELIEF ... THE ONLY STIMULANT THAT CAN NEVER BRING YOU DOWN IN TIMES OF ADVERSITIES AND OBSTACLES.

BELIEF ... THE CORE OF ALL RELIGIOUS TEACHINGS.

AFFIRM TO CONFIRM

A thought, an imagination any Form of mental activities are different forms of mental energy affirmed in varying ways. You can speak it out or think it over ... as long as they are linked to your intentions they are constructive and meaningful mental affirmations.

Focus your affirmations in the direction you want to achieve legendary deeds. As you begin to aggressively affirm ... these affirmations gets constitutionalized in you.

We are engaged in hundreds of various affirmations on a daily basis ... but then again they are rather chaotic, disorganized..they are simply random affirmations that emerges out of spontaneous responses to sensory input ... for example you are suddenly inspired by an event or a project directed toward helping and supporting the destitute ... you are emotionally moved ... your brain is at work going through a decision making process..its agreed by your mental board of directors..from this point onwards some of your thoughts imaginations are engaged working toward this spontaneous decision. These haphazardly created intentions interferes with your force of affirmations that you are directed toward your intentions of serving the whole of humanity with values of an extraordinary nature.

We should take imaginations thoughts very seriously ... just like great people do..we should think around our every thought.. we should observe our every movement our imaginations visualizations. Affirmations auto-suggestions are prayers..mystical contemplations ... just like you open up your heart to pray and worship your almighty god ... here you open up your mind and heart to be connected to your executive Authority in life ....which you can only reach through a liberalized mind. ..when affirmations takes place with this liberalized mind they transform into an energy that turns these affirmations into an automated process working toward moving you on the correct direction toward your destination.

Affirm with purpose ... with meaning ....include your heart in your thoughts and imaginations of been legendary ... of serving the world and its people, of giving your great work an undying recognition ... having your name gloriously echoing across th planet for many more centuries to come.

Be absolutely truthful in your affirmations ... you are in fact communicating here with your most deepest self which you should hold with very high dignity ... just as you do with God. Communicating to your most inner- self with a pre-occupied mind, a lack of belief or solemnity does not result in an effective communication. Its a purity to purity communique its a mind to inner mind communiqué. You need to do this in a most serene and conducive environment. For best results you need to do this as many times as possible a day.

Affirmations can also be a read-out of your life,s credo or perhaps you could create one. The most important is that all affirmations should be in line with your intentions in life.

In Tune With Your
Higher Intelligence

Energies flow into us from many avenues. Some of them are from a non-physical universal source of which we are a part of that mysterious cosmic energy.

When you are functioning from the executive chamber of your mind you are in fact also attracting this universal cosmic energy, which can empower you with a higher and powerful choice and Will that stabilizes your intentions.

Irrespective of the fact whether you are a Christian Buddhist, Muslim, Hindu or belonging to any religious beliefs, just reach out, extending your mind seeking help to confirm your creations.

Your higher intelligencies is an infinite entity and in order to attune yourself to this entity you need to be attired with the compatible mental cognitive device ... in other words totally liberalized from any form of intrusion from any of your mental faculties. This is not a mystical, religious or paranormal communication. You are attempting to draw powers from the zenith of your mind empowering you perform at extraordinary levels in all your pursuits, no matter whether they are material or spiritual goals.

Just as the world is developing the most sophisticated communication devices attempting to communicate with a species outside our planet,so should we build a mental communication device so that we get connected to our higher intelligencies. Primarily we need to build our beliefs and convictions that an intelligent faculty beyond our mind do exist ...... despite the fact that science has not been able to establish this fact.

Attuning ourselves to this channel requires a big search ... for the appropriate frequencies, and they are not visible or easily discernible. They don't get connected at your wish. They will prompt you at the most unexpected times and situations ...... what matters most is to have yourself switched- on to accept this connection identify it's attempts to prompt you and progress with them.

"It is not the strongest individual that is a winner,nor the most intelligent that excels.

But the one who has the power of adaptation to make reflective decisions in Life's dramatically changing situations."

ELMO EBERT

ABOVE ALL WE NEED PERSPIRATION

By nature we are not great believers in our own-potentials ... nor are we self- directed individuals ... now and again we are shaken up by inspirational stories of great people and motivational speeches by experts ... but lack that required self-triggering, which is of supreme importance when aspiring for legendary heights in life.

We are fired up at times of ecstasies and demoralized at times of adversities ...... we need to be pushed from within to be set in motion ... as we lack the power of SELF-DIRECTION.

We need inspiration, we need motivation ... but above all we need perspiration in mind and body ...... this perspiration of tireless exploration of our total potential ... we need a vision of such great vivacity that can see and penetrate through the fog of doubt and skepticism ... that could see the invisibilities of life ...... we need an adequate mental weapon that could conquer the impossibilities of life.

We require to have the courage and stand to shred any other material or psychological desires for a real cause ... for a real purpose in life ... you sacrifice a flamboyant present for a glorious future .... you sacrifice a waning unsustainable recognition for an undying appreciation as a legend who's name will echo across the planet for many more centuries to come.

You are dropping your ego-centric attitude replacing it with an unpretentious modest approach and attitude for a great purpose in life.

In Conclusion

Now you are a dual-personality. You still continue to be engaged in related activities to your visions and missions that has been set by you as a professional, keeping up to the same routine and action-plans that's required to take you to the intended destination in your professional world ...

Along with this transformation deep within ... you have also created "A Secret Personality"(A legend in the making)that functions at a higher level of consciousness and intelligence, attired with an adequate cognitive instrument that empowers you to aspire and accomplish legendary heights which are beyond the capacities of Power, Wealth or Fame.

THE GOOD NEWS " NO TRANSITIONAL PAINS".

Do not try to spontaneously change your beliefs and values or your existing habits

Continue your existing ways of thinking and your present Life Style.

Trying to instantly change everything in you that has got consti-tutionalized into your biological and psychological system for many years..is declaring a war within you.

Everytime you focus on change ..you are in fact creating con-flicting states of mind. And these internal or intra-psychic conflict-ing states of mind don't do you any good in changing your present disposition or re-structuring your nature. When minds are in con-flict they lose their power of pragmatism and cognition. In this state of conflict or cognitive dissonance, thought forces are de-energized weakened and so they are unable to progress towards an intended destination.

Let's think like extra-ordinary individuals ... we can change without damaging ourselves with transitional pains.

This cognitive re-structuring should be exercised with the highest degree of mental diplomacy and articulation.

These new mental activities should be introduced not as an immediate replacement of your existing mental activities ... but as an addition to already existent mental activities. This way you are not creating conflicting ground ... there is no resistance. You are at freedom to exercise these new mental activities.

Eventually, you will find yourself occupied deeper and deeper in your new positive mental activities ... and these positives will overweigh your existing intentions, thoughts and habits and a gradual harmonious transition will take place moving you to a new dimension in life.

Your newly introduced mental activities will naturally replace some of your present beliefs and convictions and will shape and fashion your mental states, personality and disposition through a natural process to remain in you like the beauty and splendor of nature, consistent and dependent like sunrise to sunset.

This transformation to a new dimension in life comes to you not by coercion but by gently nurturing your new beliefs and convictions.

THIS IS A "REAL TRANSFORMATION" *this quantum shift to a new dimension in life is made possible by the adequate mental instrument that you are now attired with, empowering you to perceive the world with a higher level of significance.*

This change is governed and controlled by your higher intelligence.

So the focus here should ideally be not on changing your existing source traits or surface traits instantaneous ... but functioning as a dual-personality working in consultation with your SECRET-PERSONALITY, introducing new traits that will grow stronger in values and contribute towards your new intentions of ......

"Moving your life to a new dimension in consciousness, Intelligence and Abilities empowering you to transform the planet to a better place to live and its people to live a life of serenity and gratification."

There are more of the unknowns in life than the knowns ...... many of our scholars have agreed on this and so do I. We get better and better on the facts that's known to us.

There are so many experts working on these known facts day after day ... but a very few exploring the unknowns of life and the dynamics surrounding it. If our concentration was stronger and deeper in these explorations ... what I'm trying to say here will be a thing of the past.

There's no reason for us to be skeptical or hesitant to move into the future. What's smart and great is not simply wait for the future but to pull it in ... to the present ... and this requires a few extraordinary individuals like you and I.

Innovation creation, revolutionary ideas has thrust the world to what it is today.If everybody simply betters on whats already known ... progression of the world in terms of consciousness,new intelligencies and abilities will come to a standstill. In other words the future will only mean that the earth rotates and keeps the calendar rolling. What we need is a world that evolves ... what we need is a Human Species that evolves day after day ...... and unless we take control of our own evolution ... we will remain in our boxes compartmentalized content and comfortable ... and perhaps let a few extraordinary people sweat in their minds and flesh to take the world to its next level.

Lets get on the field rather than been spectators watching the greats play the game of evolution and progress ... lets be a part of this great movement ... lets not be a part of the crowd from the pavillions cheering and admiring the players ... but let us be players hearing this cheering from the crowd ... inspiring and motivating us to move the world to better and higher levels of consciousness and good living.

"*BETTERING ON WHAT HAS BEEN DONE IS NOT EVOLUTIONAL ... NOT TRANSFORMATIONAL. WHAT MATTERS MOST IS THE DISCOVERY AND EXPLORATION OF THE UNKNOWNS ... THIS IS WHAT KEEPS US AND THE WORLD MOVING INTO NEW GROUND, WITH EXCITEMENT AND GLORY.*"

Just as we are attiring ourselves to move our work and our life to a new dimension ... we should also lead the world developing a "New Vision" of human possibilities and help us to meet any unforeseen challenges confidently now and ahead of us.

We are not prisoners of the past ... we are at liberty to change everything of the future, shape our destiny and bring about a new age ... an age that will recognize and experience new intelligencies and abilities empowering us with new human possibilities.

This quantum shift requires a significant change in

- How you perceive, comprehend and respond to the world,and the dynamics around it.
- A re-examination and restructuring of your beliefs convictions and attitudes toward life and work.
- Boldly accepting the fact as a species we are human ...... standing in the forefront of all nature with no limitations in potentialities.
- As an individual you are different in nature, in the sense that you capture sensory data at an elevated mental stature that extends beyond physical realities.
- And most of all you have taken control of your own evolution ...... which means that you ignite your growth by indulging yourself in compulsive Mental activities, rather than grow in biological complexities and neurological refinement as a natural process.

This drive of moving your work to a new dimension, creating an adequate cognitive instrument to perceive the world and life with a higher level of logics and understanding doesn't come overnight. Consistent focus through our mental faculties on a particular direction inevitably results in the creation of whatever you picture in your mind.

What is of paramount importance at this stage is to sustain your beliefs, your convictions and hold on to your present stage of mental stature engaging yourself with Compulsive mental activities which will help and support you to remain in an extraordinary state of mind.

When I say compulsive Mental Activities what I really mean is your world of Imaginations, Visualizations, thought processes, affirmations, auto-suggestions and all other mental activities are directed towards moving your work to a new dimension, exploring all possibilities of transforming this planet to a better place and its people to a more purposeful and meaningful living.

All your compulsive mental activities are aligned with this majestic Autonomous choice and your intentions of these legendary accomplishments.

Make that choice … use the greatest gift that you have been empowered with … That liberty to Author your life. No matter what you are today or where you are in social or financial standings. its not about where you stand right now … but what matters most is the direction you move.

Build a desire that burns like a eternal flame within you.

Put in all your energy, efforts and enthusiasm to transform your dreams to reality. It is an inexorable fact that you will ....

"Leave back a legacy the world will cherish.

Aspiring and realizing that legendary accomplishment gives you that feeling of self actualization … that sense of fulfillment. This feeling surrounds you when you have reached the summit of your life,s aspirations ...... Reaching that summit irrespective of the fact whether they are material or spiritual aspirations becomes an uphill task if you are not equipped with an adequate mental instrument.

If you are fully equipped you got yourself well grounded. If you are not adequately attired you find yourself loosing grip. Although you attempt to push on consciously you keep slipping down with lack of belief and confidence emerging out of your unconscious mind.

Ground an indomitable foundation. Adapt the correct disposition and attitude.

Primarily .... *Program your destination with your Autonomous choice and will and ignite it by visualizing yourself ecstatic at the summit with a bold and daring attitude, but still in full control of any given situation.*

The pursuit for Legendary Accomplishments remains an exclusive passion of a few extra-ordinary people who are willing to dedicate their energies and efforts in seeking the true purpose and meaning of life. We see in this great people that inexpressible passion and consistent movement toward their goals merged with their irresistible impulse to move forward.

Lets move our success stories, our Greatness beyond its mortal limitations.. ... so that the good results of our efforts and energies benefits not just a few around us but the whole of humanity, not for a few decades but deep into the future.

Make that Noble Choice to transcend to this new dimension in life that empowers you to transform the World to a better place to live ... and bring solace to its people, to live a life of fulfillment.

> *"Let our accomplishments be glorified with an undying recognition and our names echo across the planet resplendently, for many more Centuries to come "*

Elmo Ebert ... Dubai.Winter 2017.

Printed in the United States
By Bookmasters